Becoming Marriage Material

Debbie Adebayo

www.xulonpress.com

Dedication

I would like to dedicate "Becoming Marriage Material?" to my husband, Pastor Julius Adebayo. You are my covering, my pastor, my best friend and my lover. You encouraged me to complete the manuscript and get the book published. You took the time to read the manuscript and offer me invaluable feedback. You believed I could be an author and you prayed for my success. You are my testimony that those who apply the principles in this book can become marriage material and have a marriage made in heaven!

Acknowledgements

I would like to acknowledge Pastor Carlton Arthurs. For almost eighteen years you served as my Pastor. Many of the principles that I write about in this book I first learned from you. I will be forever grateful to God for the foundation your ministry laid in my life. I am marriage material today because you were faithful to be a shepherd over me.

I would like to acknowledge the Ministry Team and Partners of Singles Pleasing The Lord. Thank you for believing in the ministry and demonstrating your belief by giving your time, talents, prayer and financial support. Because of each of you I am able to minister to single adults across this country and see their lives changed. God will not forget your labor of love. My prayer for each of you who are single and desire to be married is that in your season God will prepare you to be marriage material, and for those who are already married, that your marriage will be one made in heaven.

TABLE OF CONTENTS

Preface

Through the Ministry of Singles Pleasing The Lord, God has entrusted me with the awesome responsibility of ministering to unmarried adults. Serving as founder and president of the ministry, I come in contact with single adults across this country, providing them with counsel, encouragement and prayer. One prevalent desire typically surfaces when I minister to singles: the desire to be married. This desire for marriage crosses denominational barriers, racial differences, age, gender and single status. Young adult singles who have never been married want to be married, widows who have spent the majority of their life married want to be married again, divorcees who have been traumatized by painful divorces want to remarry, and single parents raising children alone want to be married.

I have also noticed that many singles who want to be married lack the necessary insight and wisdom into Biblical truth to handle the responsibility of marriage. This deficiency deeply concerns me because of my own past and the high divorce rate in the Body of Christ. I know that desire alone is not enough to make a marriage successful and yet it seems that desire is all many single adults I've met bring to the potential union. Most lack the spiritual and emotional maturity necessary to make a marriage work. Recognizing this maturity and education as vital needs for single adults and the Body of Christ, I decided to address this problem with a book. I started writing with much enthusiasm, but as I began to reflect on my own experiences in mate selection and marriage, I began to feel that maybe writing this book was not such a good idea. Memories of my past mistakes almost stole my confidence and desire to complete this task. I began to feel that my credibility was suspect because my track record seemed to include more failures than successes.

That was when the Holy Spirit began to deal with me. He reminded me that He knew of my failures, and yet He had chosen me to author this book. He seemed to be telling me that He wanted me to use my mistakes and failures as building blocks to help other single adults avoid the mistakes I had made. God can turn our mistakes into blessings for others. To convince me, the Holy Spirit led me to the book of Ruth and reminded me that He chose Naomi to introduce Ruth and Boaz—an introduction that led to one of history's most romantic and significant marriages. He did not select Naomi because of any great relationship wisdom. Quite the contrary, Naomi selected as her husband Ebimelech who—when he was faced with the pressures of famine in Bethlehem—led her out of God's will and into a heathen land.

Because Ebimelech failed to trust God during hard times, he entered into compromise, which in turn led to Naomi's two sons marrying heathen women. Eventually Naomi's husband and two sons died, leaving her impoverished and grief-stricken and in the land of Moab, outside God's will. Clearly Naomi's marriage resume left something to be desired. Yet God chose her because she pushed past her pain and chose to move forward, allowing God to work in her circumstances for good. The Spirit of God gave Naomi the wisdom Ruth needed for a successful courtship and marriage. God used Naomi's influence to bring together Boaz, a man known for his cash and character, and Ruth, a virtuous woman. In the process, Naomi gained a new family.

God used Naomi's example to convince me to author this book, because I am intimately acquainted with the devastation that afflicts those who don't follow Biblical marriage principles. I know what doesn't work. I know the pitfalls, danger zones and warning signals that will turn a marriage desire into a destiny-altering tragedy. You don't have to make the same mistakes I made with my desire for marriage. One set of mistakes is enough for both of us. As you read this book, permit God's Spirit to prepare you to be marriage material and take your desire for a marriage partner and turn it into reality. Thanks to the Biblical principles in this book, on July 16, 2005, I married God's awesome man for me and I am discovering the marital success God intends for everyone he has called to be married.

Introduction

M ost unmarried adults have a strong desire to be married. I know I did. There were times in my life when the desire to be married nearly consumed and controlled me. The desire to be married comes straight from God's heart; He created the institution of marriage. However, desire for marriage and readiness for marriage are two totally different issues. You can have a desire for something you're not ready for. We will discuss the various degrees of desire as we progress through this book. Readiness, on the other hand, indicates you are prepared for something. Readiness can occur in several different levels, and we will discuss the levels of readiness as well. Keeping these two points (desire and readiness) in mind it becomes vital that every unmarried adult not only consider their desire for marriage, but also their readiness for marriage. Before you tie the knot and take the plunge, take time to thoroughly examine the question: "Are You Marriage Material?"

This book will help you make that assessment so that your desire and your readiness are in agreement.

If you will prayerfully read this book, honestly evaluate your readiness and yield your desire for a marriage partner to God, in your season He will give you the desire of your heart – a marriage partner, and a marriage made in heaven or a fulfilled and productive single life.

Chapter One

My Story

For as long as I can remember I have always wanted to be married. My earliest recollections of dreams and aspirations as a young child were that one day I would get married and have children. My favorite playtime activity as a little girl growing up was playing house. I would always pretend I was a wife and would cook dinner for my husband, using toy pots and pans. I would take care of our children, using my dolls or sometimes just roll a magazine together and hold it securely in my arms, like I was caring for my infant.

As I grew older that desire became even stronger. Now I did not play house, but I dreamed that one day I would meet someone very special and we would fall passionately in love with one another. I believed we would get engaged and have a big, beautiful wedding. I would browse through bridal magazines, selecting dresses that I wanted to wear. Sometimes I would daydream, seeing myself in a form fitting pure white lace gown with a very long cathedral train. There were times when I was so consumed with this desire that I would practice marching down the aisle. I would select songs, turn my stereo on with the volume very loud, pretend to hold my bridal bouquet, grasp my arm as if my daddy was holding it and march down the center aisle of my apartment. I would imagine the pastor pronouncing us (my man and I) husband and wife and my new husband giving me a passionate kiss. We would recess down the aisle together, and then I would switch my daydream to the reception where all eyes would be glued on us as we danced our first dance to a sensual love song.

Of all the dreams and aspirations I have ever had, the desire to be married has always been the strongest. God eventually did give me this daydream almost exactly like I used to imagine, but not until after I had experienced a very troubled marriage and an excruciatingly painful divorce. No one could have had a stronger desire than I had for marriage, and yet that desire alone did not prepare me to become marriage material. Let me share with you in greater detail the type of life I lived prior to getting married the first time. I think it will point out why it is so important to have more than a desire to be married, but also to *be ready* to be married.

While attending college, and studying to be a registered nurse, my main concern was graduating and starting a career. My grandparents had instilled that goal in me from the time I was a very small child. Consequently, I was not focused on meeting someone to marry. I dated for companionship and fun but there was never any talk of marriage. I wanted to graduate, get a good paying job, get my own apartment and buy my own car. After graduating, I accomplished these goals just as I had planned. I also managed to get myself into a great deal of debt to get all the things I felt I deserved after making many sacrifices to complete my degree. But my career choice, new car and apartment as well as a weekly weekend shopping spree did not bring me fulfillment.

Even though I spent time socializing with my friends and frequent casual dating, I still had a void. I had an incredible amount of loneliness during this time. I tried to keep myself busy every minute of the day until it was time to go to bed so

I did not have to deal with the emptiness that the single life was bringing me. I hated being by myself and being single. I assumed that getting married must be what was missing from my life. The fact that many of my closest high school and college girl friends were getting married only increased my desire. Every time I participated in a wedding as a bridesmaid, or attended a shower watching lingerie gifts being opened, my already intense desire for marriage increased. I would pretend to smile and be happy, but deep inside I was jealous and envious of my friends' happiness. Age 25 passed, then age 26 and 27, and still I was not married. Feelings of anxiety and worry began to overtake me as I began to contemplate the idea that I might not get married. I was apprehensive and fearful that the one thing I had always wanted and dreamed of would never happen. You could tell my anxiety was getting the best of me because of what I was willing to do to get and keep a man. Although sexually active with guys while in college, the amount of sexual activity that I became involved in increased as my search for a husband intensified. My desire for marriage had turned into a hunt for a husband. I was developing the mindset that I had to do whatever it took to address this unmet need in my life.

During this time I attended church regularly. My grandparents had raised me in the church, and so church attendance was an important part of my life. But my search for a husband was much broader than eligible men in the church, it included wherever I could find an eligible single man, the church, the nightclub, the laundromat, grocery store or riding in the car. I remember one occasion when I was in the car with my girlfriend. We pulled up at a stoplight and I looked over in the car that was stopped in the other lane. I smiled at the very handsome guy in the driver's seat of the other car and we began to talk.

He asked me how I was doing and I replied fine. He said you can say that again, you sure are fine. He then invited my friend and me to join him and his friend at his apartment. My friend and I agreed to the meeting and followed these two guys to their apartment. Both my friend and I started relationships with these guys. These relationships landed me regular weekend sexual meetings and ultimately a broken heart and my friend ended up with a sexually transmitted disease. Obviously Jesus was not the center of my life. I did not identify Him as my Savior and definitely not my Lord. I lived my life doing what I wanted to do when I wanted to do it.

At the age of 25 I had a genuine salvation experience. Filled with unmet needs and dying to get married I decided to give Jesus a chance to help me. I was a member of the church I got saved in for almost two years before I accepted Jesus as my Savior. On the third Sunday in April of 1980, I responded to the pastor's call to come to the altar and get closer to Jesus. I walked down the aisle hoping that maybe this was the answer to my empty life—I gave my heart to Jesus. I would not call my initial conversion dramatic or emotional, but I could tell immediately a change had taken place in my life. I began to live my life with an obvious awareness of the Holy Spirit. After getting saved, however, I did not begin to grow in my understanding of God, His Word and His desire to direct my life. Jesus became my Savior, I knew my sins were forgiven, but it was almost eleven years later before he became my Lord. Because Jesus was Savior, and the Holy Spirit lived inside me, whenever I became involved in sexual sin there was an immediate conviction that what I was doing was wrong. Before getting saved I could have sex with a man and not feel one ounce of guilt, but after that third Sunday in April I felt very guilty every time I had sex outside marriage. It would feel great during the foreplay and actual intercourse but afterwards I hated myself and knew that Jesus was very displeased. The guilt only complicated my life and gave me another reason to hurry up and get married – so I could have sex and not feel guilty.

What I needed in my life at this point was good, solid teaching from the Bible so I could put my single life, sexual drive and desire for marriage in proper perspective (just like the teaching you are about to be exposed to as you continue to read this book). Instead of being rescued from this drama by the Word of God I continued to try and satisfy my needs with my own knowledge, totally driven by my desires. My craving for sex and marriage and my inability to deal with my loneliness was leading me down a path of deception and destruction.

During this time my grandmother passed away. My grandmother, whom I called "Bigmama," was very special to me. She was a source of spiritual strength, and I believed in her ability to pray for me. Whenever I needed God to move in my life, I always called "Bigmama" and asked her to pray. When she died it was like one of the foundational pieces to my life had been taken away. I became depressed and felt like God had not kept his promise to me. I had asked God to heal my grandmother and believed that I was exercising faith for that to happen, and still she died. I was confused, hurt and very disappointed with God. It was shortly after her death and while going through this very difficult grieving process I met my first husband.

I worked the evening shift in a county hospital as a registered nurse on a pediatric unit. He was a handsome security guard, fair in complexion with beautiful curly black hair. We met and exchanged casual conversation from time to time. The more we talked, the more I looked forward to his evening patrol to check the security of our unit. Initially, I had no romantic interest in him and surely did not see him as someone I would consider marrying. My desire was to marry a professional, such as a lawyer, doctor or accountant. But I did enjoy talking with him, and he was very handsome. He was easy to talk to and I was going through a lot at that time. Many of my closest friends were already married and involved with their families (I was 28), and so I enjoyed his friendship. Early in the relationship I let him know I was saved and was endeavoring to live a saved life. I really was trying very hard to not have sex with men at this time. He admitted that he was not saved but would like to get to know more about God and the Bible. He shared with me the very difficult life he had, beginning with watching his mother and father get divorced as a young child, physical abuse by a stepfather, and spending time in the Vietnam War, which left him addicted to heroin and sexually promiscuous. He stated that he was able to kick the heroin addiction, but he still smoked cigarettes. He stated that he had been married three times before, and because of this and ongoing promiscuity he had nine children by nine different women. He also shared that because of child support his finances were severely challenged and he currently lived with his father in order to be able to survive. I listened to his story and was moved with compassion. He needed help and two years into my salvation experience I wanted to help him by telling him about Jesus and how Jesus could help him. He seemed very receptive. Shortly after witnessing to him and telling him that giving his heart to Jesus would make a dramatic difference in his life I led him in the sinner's prayer, and it seemed as if he became a Christian. This experience brought me great joy and a degree of fulfillment I had never known. This man seemed to take away the loneliness and misery I was having with the single life. His response to God energized me and made me excited about living. My depression over my grandmother's death left. He began to go to church with me and listen to Christian music. He got baptized, filled with the Holy Spirit and began to demonstrate what I thought were signs of God's intimate involvement in his life. His conversion seemed very real, and it caused my feelings to change for him. I began to develop a very strong romantic interest in him. Suddenly it didn't matter that he was a security guard; I began to see him as a man of God. As we started to date and spend long periods of time alone together the sexual passion began to ignite. We would leave the hospital where we both work together around midnight, order a pizza, go to my apartment and study the Bible. It was not long before our late night Bible studies and pizza parties became all night passionate sexual encounters. We would come to my apartment with the intention of reading the Bible together and praying and the Bible would end up on the floor and we would end up in my bed. I had never experienced sex like this before, he knew how to turn me on physically, but the guilt I experienced after each encounter was tormenting. He said he felt guilty too. After about sixteen months of this we agreed we loved one another and in order to be able to enjoy one another without guilt we should get married. We felt strongly that God had brought us together. We got engaged and four months later we were married.

Several things happened during this four-month period prior to our wedding that should have stopped this tragedy from occurring, but because I was consumed with the desire to be married and attached to the sexual passion nothing could stop me. First, a month after we announced our engagement my mother died very unexpectedly. She passed out at church while giving a testimony of God's goodness and three days later she was dead. My mother and I had become very close after the death of my grandmother, and I considered her my very best friend. I was devastated by her death and the pain caused me to want to hurry up and get married and be with this man. I needed him more than ever now. All my other support systems were gone – my grandparents and mother were dead and my closet friends were married, so I felt like

God was sending this man to take their places. I soon discovered after this that one of the worst mistakes you can make is to make major life decisions such as getting married after a significant tragedy in your life. The impact of the tragedy clouds your ability to execute sound judgment.

We also went for counseling at the church we attended. The senior pastor met with us, and when he discovered the details of my first husband's life, including the previous marriages and children, he advised us to reconsider our decision. He said we should take a month and pray again and make sure we were hearing from God. I remember being furious when I left that counseling session. I thought, *"How could he question our ability to hear from God?"* I remember thinking, *"I know what his past is, and God is bringing us together so I can help him."* Not once did I ever think my ability to accurately assess this situation was being significantly hindered by my out-of-control sexual passion for him. A month later we went back and informed this pastor that we still believed it was God bringing us together and we wanted to move forward with our marriage plans. He agreed to permit one of the assistant pastors in the church to perform the wedding ceremony. As I look back on that now I wish he would have refused to marry us. I also want to add that during the counseling session there was no mention of our sexual activity during our courtship. The Pastor didn't ask and we didn't volunteer any information about the sexual activity we were involved in. There were no questions asked about our finances and how we were going to make it. The only concern that was mentioned was my fiancé's past, and my deception was too deep at that point to be moved by that. In my heart I honestly believed God was bringing us together so I could help him. I had it all planned: I was going to help him get a better paying job once we were married, and also help him raise his kids. In fact, one of his sons was already planning to move in with us after the wedding ceremony. It never entered my mind once, that I should have let him get a better-paying joy before we were married.

Then, about six weeks before our wedding, my fiancé's youngest daughter, who was less than one year old, was physically abused by her mother and died. This was a devastating blow to both of us. You would think it would have served as a wake-up call, that maybe we should at least put the marriage on hold. I remember my fiancé's best friend came to me at the funeral of this child and suggested that I may want to go away for a weekend alone and really reconsider what I was about to do. I refused, stating I knew exactly what I was about to do and I believed God was leading me.

About a week before the wedding, the Pastor from the church that I grew up in my hometown called me and said he felt the Lord wanted him to warn me that the man I was about to marry was not God's choice and I should stop the wedding. I thanked him but told him I believed I was hearing from God and planned to move forward with the wedding.

The day before our wedding we had a violent argument and my fiancé cursed me in a way that stunned me. It really frightened me and for the first time caused me to question my decision. But a day before the wedding I had too much at stake to stop anything at this point.

All these events could have served as red flags for me to reconsider my actions, but my desire for marriage and sex was so strong that I completely ignored every red flag, no matter how major it was and who tried to bring it to me.

Six months after I was married I began to experience hell on this earth. The marriage was marked by mental and physical abuse. I will never forget one of the first episodes of abuse. We were having a heated argument about where my husband had been and why he was coming home so much later than he promised. I expressed my anger and frustration at him by speaking negatively about one of his children, he hit me, leaving me with a black eye. I was stunned and deeply wounded physically and emotionally. Over time I discovered his blatant adultery, use of pornography and smoking marijuana and drinking alcohol. I was brokenhearted and devastated. I was also the primary financial provider, and I was overwhelmed at trying to hold down a full-time job as a Director of Nursing, manage our home, raise his children and deal with his ungodly lifestyle. Although I developed a very special relationship with one of my stepson's (more about this later in the book), the help I thought I was going to give my husband with childrearing with most of his children became a nightmare as I realized that raising someone else's child takes a special grace that only God can give, and there were many times when I did not have it.

My first husband's love for Christ and desire to be involved in the church seemed to all but disappear, and within a year I found myself begging him to go to church only to have him refuse. I remember wanting him to go with me so bad that I would ask for him to go to church with me as my birthday and Christmas gifts. Most of the time he would not, and I remember sitting in my local church many Sundays a lonely, hurting woman praying that God would change this man I had married.

Seven years later this very troubled marriage ended in divorce that left me emotionally traumatized and suicidal. When I left the marriage I felt like I was running for my life. While he was at work, I left our home in the middle of the night, taking as many of my belongings as I could carry. I was fearful that if I tried to tell him I was leaving he would harm me and not let me go. While packing and removing a family picture from the wall, my stepson discovered that a "peeping–Tom" hole had been built in our home that allowed someone to view our bathroom from our family room. When my stepson showed me this, I began to realize that I had no idea the person I had really married and what his lifestyle may have entailed. I felt empty and deeply betrayed. I left my husband a note explaining that more than he realized I wanted our marriage to work out, but I could not continue to live under these conditions. I told him that I would come back to him and work on our marriage if he would agree to counseling and stop the adultery. Six months later he told me that he did not want to be married, but wanted to be free to date other people. We filed for a divorce. Shortly after the divorce was final, he remarried.

When we separated, the pain was so intense it felt like someone took the world's sharpest dagger and ripped my chest open, snatched my heart out of my chest and began to stab me in my heart as hard and as fast as possible. It took years to recover from this devastation, but I eventually did receive God's healing mercy and a new beginning.

What happened? How did my pure, innocent childhood desire for marriage turn into a hideous destructive bondage? The simple answer is, I had a desire for marriage but I was not ready for marriage. Just because you really want something does not mean you are qualified to handle it. That desire led me into deception and devastation. I now know that all the desire in the world will not produce readiness for marriage. Readiness is something you must deliberately develop. If I would have spent as much time making myself ready for marriage as I did pursuing a marriage partner I would have had what God wanted to give me the first time. I also believe my sexual desire—rather than God—was directing my path. I had not learned how to recognize God's voice and follow His direction, one of the things that qualifies you to be ready for marriage. I did not hear God telling me, "No, this is not the mate I have chosen for you." All I heard were my sexual desires and emotions telling me: "This has to be God; it feels too good not to be." My emotions and sexual desires were so strong they would not let me use my common sense. I had a Masters Degree in Business Administration and a good paying job, but I did not have the wisdom to deal with my desire for marriage.

My prayer is that no single adult who reads this book will ever make the mistake that I made. Many of you after reading about my mistake may feel you are too smart to make the same mistakes, and yet the divorce statistics for marriages in the Body of Christ are significant enough that it is obvious that many single people lack the necessary material to make a marriage work. I encourage you to read each chapter in this book carefully, allowing it to show you what it takes to prepare for marriage so your story will be different than my first marriage. God ultimately did give me a new beginning and an awesome husband and marriage (I will share that testimony later in the book) but before he could bless me I had to become marriage material.

Chapter Two

Sex, Money and Loneliness

The most common reasons people get married are the worst reasons to get married. Most people enter marriage without a solid understanding of Biblical truth. As you can tell from my story, I did not have this understanding. I approached marriage with a very selfish agenda. I wanted to get married because of what was in it for me.

Listed below are the four most common reasons people get married:

1. To have sexual intercourse
2. To alleviate loneliness
3. To enhance self-esteem
4. To receive financial assistance

These reasons aren't inherently wrong, but meeting sexual, financial and companionship needs are not the building blocks for a successful marriage. They are fringe benefits of marriage. But you can't build a solid foundation on a fringe benefit. All you need do is look at the current divorce rate in the Body of Christ to validate this. The rest of this chapter will be devoted to examining these reasons.

"I Want to Get Married So I Can Have Sex"

Like I did, many people desire marriage because their sexual drive is dominating and driving them. Uppermost in the mind of these singles is the desire for sex. The media has had a profound impact on creating this desire for sexual intimacy. The normal God-given human sexual drive is strong. Unmarried Christian adults must exercise self-control, temperance and discipline over this sexual drive. The degree of self-control necessary is directly proportionate to the degree of stimulation you have been exposed to. Unmarried adults who have engaged in promiscuous sexual activity have to fight to gain discipline in this area. Widowed and divorced people may also have difficulty gaining control over their sexual drive. I discovered after my marriage ended the first time that my sexual drive did not understand that I was divorced. It did not come to divorce court with me, and when I came home from divorce court it wanted the same degree of attention that it had while I was married. I had a real battle in this area and it took diligent, deliberate effort on my part and God's grace to get the victory. God did ultimately give me the victory and I remained celibate for fourteen years until God sent me Julius to marry and he lived without sex five years prior to our marriage. But I will be the first to admit this was not easy.

Rather than pay the price to develop self-control, many single adults opt to find a marriage partner. Great sex is one of the awesome benefits of marriage. Proverbs 5:18-19 says, "Let your fountain [of human life] be blessed [with the rewards of fidelity], and rejoice in the wife of your youth. Let her be as the loving hind and pleasant doe [tender, gentle, attractive]—let her bosom satisfy you at all times, and always be transported with delight in her love." The seventh chapter of the Song of Solomon gives a very graphic depiction of lovemaking between a husband and wife, indicating obvious enjoyment and pleasure.

[THEN HER companions began noticing and commenting on the attractiveness of her person] How beautiful are your feet in sandals, O queenly maiden! Your rounded limbs are like jeweled chains, the work of a master hand. Your body is like a round goblet in which no mixed wine is wanting. Your abdomen is like a heap of wheat set about with lilies. Your two breasts are like two fawns, the twins of a gazelle. Your neck is like a tower of ivory, your eyes like the pools of Heshbon by the gate of Bath-rabbim. Your nose is like the tower of Lebanon which looks toward Damascus. Your head crowns you like Mount Carmel, and the hair of your head like purple. [Then seeing the king watching the girl in absorbed admiration, the speaker added] The king is held captive by its tresses. [The king came forward, saying] How fair and how pleasant you are, O love, with your delights! Your stature is like that of a palm tree, and your bosom like its clusters [of dates, declared the king]. I resolve that I will climb the palm tree; I will grasp its branches. Let your breasts be like clusters of the grapevine, and the scent of your breath like apples, And your kisses like the best wine— [then the Shulammite interrupted] that goes down smoothly and sweetly for my beloved [shepherd, kisses] gliding over his lips while he sleeps! [She proudly said] I am my beloved's, and his desire is toward me! [She said] Come, my beloved! Let us go forth into the field, let us lodge in the villages. Let us go out early to the vineyards and see whether the vines have budded, whether the grape blossoms have opened, and whether the pomegranates are in bloom.

There I will give you my love. The mandrakes give forth fragrance, and over our doors are all manner of choice fruits, new and old, which I have laid up for you, O my beloved!

From these passages you can see the Word of God clearly establishes God created sex for married people to enjoy, but it does not indicate that it will make a marriage successful.

1 Corinthians 7:9 says, "But if they have not self-control (restraint of their passions), they should marry. For it is better to marry than to be aflame [with passion and tortured continually with ungratified desire]." In other words, the Apostle Paul says, if you are not willing to pay the price to develop self-control, you should get married. If you don't, you will be tortured with ungratified sexual desire. You may be quick to latch onto this verse as your primary reason for getting married. But while marriage may provide sexual gratification, if you are not ready to handle the other responsibilities and pressures of marriage, you will struggle to have a successful marriage and there is a strong possibility that your marriage will end up failing anyway. Then the very problem you were trying to solve will be back to torment you. I have firsthand knowledge of this. I was sexually active with my first husband before marriage, and the sex was great. I could hardly wait to get married because then I could have sex and not feel guilty. But I soon discovered that sex did not help pay bills, establish trust, develop a solid spiritual foundation or enhance our ability to communicate.

During my first marriage I often had great sex within a very bad marriage. I could finish an awesome sexual climax and return to poor communication, arguments about finances and distrust about my spouse's activities. Great sex did not give me a great marriage. And lust does not stop after you say, "I do." I masturbated before I got married and after I got married, even though I was having sex on a regular basis.

Why, because I was being influenced by a spirit of lust. Marriage does not cure lust. Lust is dealt with by deliverance and development of the fruit of the spirit self-control. We needed more than sex to make our marriage work. We needed a revelation of God's purpose of marriage and the grace to live it out. Sex provided neither. On many different occasions I have had married people share with me they got married so they could deal with the tremendous sexual pressure from the single life. But now they wished they had not, because the married life is so difficult.

If you are willing to pay the price to develop self-control you will be a much better person and therefore a much better marriage partner. Galatians 5:22-23 identifies self-control as a fruit of the Spirit. "But the fruit of the [Holy] Spirit [the work which His presence within accomplishes] is love, joy (gladness), peace, patience (an even temper, forbearance), kindness, goodness (benevolence), faithfulness, gentleness (meekness, humility), self-control (self-restraint, continence). Against such things there is no law [that can bring a charge]." There is a seed of each of these fruit in every believer at the time they accept Jesus as Savior and Lord. But the seed must be cultivated, and that requires time and effort. You must be willing to pay the price. It's easier to just get married. Marriage may provide short-term pleasure and benefits, but in the long run, if you marry the wrong person the short-term sexual gratification will not compensate for the ongoing problems of the marriage.

Marrying someone who is not willing to cultivate self-control may affect other aspects of your marriage. If you can't discipline your sexual drive, can you discipline your appetite or manage money? When you have self-control you can exert influence not only over your sexual organs, but also over your finances, your tongue and your appetite. Failure to develop self-control in any of these areas may be problematic for any marriage. Many marriages today are marked by debt, financial mismanagement, verbal abuse, bodies that have lost their sexual appeal, and nagging, because one or both of the spouses lack self-control. There is also the very strong possibility that if you cannot control your sexual drive before marriage, you will not be able to control it after you are married. Many people who fornicate prior to marriage commit adultery after marriage because they don't have self-control. So if you believe sex alone is going to provide you with a happy marriage, you may want to think again.

I am Tired of Being Lonely: I Want To Get Married!

In my story I told you that after I graduated from college and began to live alone I experienced a great deal of loneliness. This loneliness is one of the major reasons I wanted to get married. I could not stand the void and empty feeling that being by myself left me with.

Genesis 2:18 reveals that God approached Adam and said (essentially), "Adam you are alone; I want you to get married." Marriage was not Adam's selfish desire in response to unbearable loneliness; it was God's plan for Adam's life. I, on the other hand, was always telling God about my loneliness and asking Him to send me a marriage partner to address it.

The definition I give loneliness is this: "The negative emotion you choose to ascribe to the state of being alone." Many single adults are sad, depressed and even suicidal when they are alone. Adam was alone, but neither God nor Adam had defined that as a negative condition.

The original Hebrew word for *alone* in Genesis 2:18 comes from the word "bad." The King James Version Old Testament Hebrew Lexicon indicates that this word has several meanings. Neither of these meanings implies loneliness. One meaning is "a part." If we go back and replace the word alone with "a part," we discover that God was not responding to Adam's loneliness. God was responding to the fact that Adam was only a part, and as an isolated part he could not carry out God's will, which was to be fruitful and multiply and establish the family of God. Adam represented just one part of the entire family that God desired. The Body of Christ today is made up of many parts, but it started with just one part, and that one part was Adam. 1 Corinthian 12: 14-24,27 says,

> For the body does not consist of one limb or organ but of many. If the foot should say, Because I am not the hand, I do not belong to the body, would it be therefore not [a part] of the body? If the ear should say, Because I am not the eye, I do not belong to the body, would it be therefore not [a part] of the body? If the whole body were an eye, where [would be the sense of] hearing? If the whole body were an ear, where [would be the sense of] smell? But as it is, God has placed and arranged the limbs and organs in the body, each [particular one] of them, just as He wished and saw fit and with the best adaptation. But if [the whole] were all a single organ, where would the body be? And now there are [certainly] many limbs and organs, but a single body. And the eye is not able to say to the hand, I have no need of you, nor again the head to the feet, I have no need of you. But instead, there is [absolute] necessity for the parts of the body that are considered the more weak. And those [parts] of the body which we consider rather ignoble are [the very parts] which we invest with additional honor, and our unseemly parts and those unsuitable for exposure are treated with seemliness (modesty and decorum), Which our more present-able parts do not require. But God has so adjusted (mingled, harmonized, and subtly proportioned the

parts of) the whole body, giving the greater honor and richer endowment to the inferior parts which lack [apparent importance]. Now you [collectively] are Christ's body and [individually] you are members of it, each part severally and distinct [each with his own place and function].

Adam was the first part of God's family, but God needed Adam married in order to have the many parts He desired.

God was not responding to Adam's loneliness when He brought Eve into his life. God was focused on His overall Kingdom agenda and Adam's role in accomplishing it. For Adam, marriage was God's method for accomplishing His will in the earth. God's will was to have a family made up of many parts. Is your marriage desire rooted in accomplishing God's kingdom agenda? Do you understand how your marriage desire will enhance God's Kingdom and accomplish God's will on earth? Has God spoken to you, as He did to Adam, and informed you that it is not good for you to remain alone, because if you remain alone, He will not be able to accomplish his will for your life? Has God informed you that in order for you to have His desired impact on His Kingdom you must be married?

Adam did not see himself as alone, because God was with Him. Adam had never been around other people, and so he did not know what it meant to have relationship with anyone but God. He knew that God was always present with him. Jesus knew He was not alone even when all his disciples left Him, because God was with Him. John 16:32 says, "But take notice, the hour is coming and it has arrived, when you will all be dispersed and scattered, every man to his own home, leaving Me alone. Yet I am not alone, because the Father is with me." In order to get where Jesus was — about being alone — you must grow in your understanding of God's character attributes. If you really recognize that God is omnipotent, omniscient, altogether lovely, awe-inspiring, and profoundly impressive, you can become overwhelmed with who He is when you enter His presence, and He can captivate you and arrest your attention as He reveals Himself to you. When that happens, loneliness will be diminished and alleviated. After my first marriage ended I began to seek God with a passion by studying His Word, reading good Christian books, participating in regular prayer and praise at church and home and intense, active involvement in my local church. As I sought him, I began to discover Him and His ways and my loneliness left. I grew in my understanding of God to the point that I rarely dealt with loneliness and when I did it was because I took my focus off God. God arrested my attention and filled my voids. As God became my first and ultimate source of fulfillment, I did not need a husband to take away my loneliness. When I married Julius I did not marry him because I was lonely. I married him because he was God's choice for me.

"Having A Marriage Partner Will Help Me Feel Better About Myself!"

People who are comfortable being alone and intimate with God are satisfied and fulfilled as individuals. They are not seeking validation of their worth or fulfillment from another person, because they have already received fulfillment from God. They are prepared to enhance another person's life. When you enhance someone's life you are improving what is already good, not meeting a void, eliminating lack, fixing a problem or addressing a need. You are adding value to something that is good all by itself! Single adults who are driven to marriage because of loneliness are typically not just lonely but also insecure, anxious, miserable, in debt (because they think that if they spend enough money their loneliness will go away) obese, have low self-esteem and are seeking someone to validate their worth. They bring these needs to a marriage relationship believing that it is the responsibility of their spouse to meet these needs.

My first marriage demonstrated how sadly mistaken and disappointed we are when we discover a person cannot address these needs. I thought my first husband was going to take my unfulfilled life and make it complete. Instead, because neither one of us had become marriage material before marrying, I was more frustrated than I was while I was single. The one thing I thought would make my life better ended up giving me more heartache, disappointment and frustration than I had before I got married. In reality I was being unfair to my first husband because I looked to him to meet needs that only God should meet. God did not design a marriage partner to make me complete—He wanted to do that Himself.

God is not going to give you a spouse to help you feel good about yourself. If He cannot convince you of your value by sending His only Son to shed His precious pure blood for you, I assure you no human being will enhance your self-esteem. Prior to my first marriage my self-esteem came through the validation I received from other people, particularly the opposite sex. I dressed seductively, wearing something form-fitting to expose all my body parts that I knew would attract the attention of men. This attention made me feel good about myself. I dated men even when they mistreated me because I thought having a date or a boyfriend made me someone special. If I was not receiving validation I felt insecure and struggled with my self-worth. This unhealthy self-esteem led me down the path of a selecting the wrong marriage partner. I didn't know who I was and how valuable I was to God and His Kingdom; therefore I was incapable of selecting the right person to marry. God had to first reveal to me who I was in Him before He could tell me the person He wanted me to marry. God did that for me by leading me to his Word. For months I meditated on Psalms 139:14-18, allowing the Holy Spirit to convince me that it was true.

> I will confess and praise You for You are fearful and wonderful and for the awful wonder of my birth! Wonderful are Your works, and that my inner self knows right well. My frame was not hidden from You when I was being formed in secret [and] intricately and curiously wrought [as if embroidered with various colors] in the depths of the earth [a region of darkness and mystery]. Your eyes saw my unformed substance, and in Your book all the days [of my life] were written before ever they took shape, when as yet there was none of them. How precious and weighty also are Your thoughts to me, O God! How vast is the sum of them! If I could count them, they would be more in number than the sand. When I awoke, [could I count to the end] I would still be with You.

I began to understand the care and attention to detail that God had given to my creation and my current life. Especially as I reflected on verse 17 I realized God was thinking precious and weighty thoughts about me that outnumbered the grains of the sand of the sea. I began to realize what a special person I was, without a boyfriend or husband—and without exposing my body. This insight was freeing to me. To cement God's viewpoint of me in my mind, on a business trip while still working in corporate America, I traveled to California and had the awesome favor of getting a hotel room with a patio that opened right to a sandy beach on the Pacific Ocean. During some free time I decided to take a walk and enjoy the beauty. I got my Walkman cassette player, turned on my praise and worship music, placed my earphones in my ear, took off my shoes and began to walk barefoot along the beach. The sun was warm and it made the sand warm, and as I walked the sand rolled on my feet and felt so good. As I was enjoying these moments the Holy Spirit began to speak. He told me to pick up a hand full of sand. I did and then He asked me if I could count the grains. I thought to myself, I can't, and then He reminded me of verse 17. He said every grain of sand you have in your hand represents a precious weighty thought I am thinking about you right now. You can't even count them. I was overjoyed and overwhelmed as I realized God's opinion of me.

I also began to speak on a regular basis what Proverbs 31 taught me. I confessed until I believed it that I was a virtuous, intelligent capable woman of God, more valuable than diamonds, rubies and emeralds—worth the blood of Jesus. As I heard my own lips say that I began to believe it, and as I began to believe it I began to carry myself as a confident assured woman of God who deserved God's best. I noticed that as I felt differently about myself, people—in particular men—began to treat me differently. Men began to have a degree of respect for me that I had not experienced when I was trying to seduce them to pay attention to me. It was as if they knew I was a very special woman, and they did not approach me loosely and unwisely anymore. When Julius contacted me the first time to express his interest in me and to seek my permission to date, he confirmed the value that I had permitted the Word of God and the Holy Spirit to establish in my heart. He shared with me that as he prayed about me the Lord spoke to him and told him that I was one of His most valuable jewels. That filled me with joy, and I knew it was true because God had been telling me that for years until I believed it.

It's Hard To Make It On Just One Income – I Think I'll Get Married!

We have heard the stories of women who set out to manipulate wealthy men into marriage and single brothers who marry women with money so that they can advance their careers and become financially established. There are also those situations where a girl is raised by a father who did not adequately provide for her and so as soon as she is old enough she marries the first man that comes along with a job in an effort to get the financial security and good life she saw on television but was never able to experience growing up. What these singles fail to realize is that God did not design marriage as His method for financial stability. Genesis 2:8-14 shows us that Adam didn't need Eve to help bring financial abundance into his life.

> And the Lord God planted a garden toward the east, in Eden [delight]; and there He put the man whom He had formed (framed, constituted). And out of the ground the Lord God made to grow every tree that is pleasant to the sight or to be desired—good (suitable, pleasant) for food; the tree of life also in the center of the garden, and the tree of the knowledge of [the difference between] good and evil and blessing and calamity. Now a river went out of Eden to water the garden; and from there it divided and became four [river] heads. The first is named Pishon; it is the one flowing around the whole land of Havilah, where there is gold. The gold of that land is of high quality; bdellium (pearl?) and onyx stone are there. The second river is named Gihon; it is the one flowing around the whole land of Cush. The third river is named Hiddekel [the Tigris]; it is the one flowing east of Assyria. And the fourth river is the Euphrates.

God gave Adam gold before He gave him Eve. Some people believe marriage is the motivation single adults need to get their finances in order, but actually the Word of God reveals through Adam that a single adult should have their finances in order before they enter marriage. I believe successful financial management at a very minimum should include a regular income that permits you with ease to tithe and give offerings, pay your living expenses and save and grow 10 percent of your income. Ideally, this income should come from employment God has called you to that you find fulfillment in. This is basic financial management.

Not only that; God has not designed marriage as His methodology for financial increase. God has designed seed-time and harvest as His method to bring financial increase into the lives of believers. The Word of God in 2 Corinthians 9: 6-8 says:

> [Remember] this: he who sows sparingly and grudgingly will also reap sparingly and grudgingly, and he who sows generously that blessings may come to someone] will also reap generously and with blessings. Let each one [give] as he has made up his own mind and purposed in his heart, not reluctantly or sorrowfully or under compulsion, for God loves (He takes pleasure in, prizes above other things, and is unwilling to abandon or to do without) a cheerful (joyous, "prompt to do it") giver [whose heart is in his giving]. And God is able to make all grace (every favor and earthly blessing) come to you in abundance, so that you may always and under all circumstances and whatever the need be self-sufficient [possessing enough to require no aid or support and furnished in abundance for every good work and charitable donation].

The best way for single adults to improve their finances is to genuinely want money for the right reason. As your motive for financial increase is purified, the wisdom and discipline necessary to handle financial increase will begin to manifest in your life. After my divorce I was over $10,000 dollars in credit card debt. As I began to seek the Kingdom of God first instead of a new marriage partner, God put such a love in my heart for Him and His Kingdom that He provided me with the financial resources to pay off all my debt and blessed me so that I gave tens of thousands of dollars over the tithe into God's work. When I wanted money for the right reason and when I was ready and willing to live my life to please God, God sent me money. When I married Julius, I brought no debt into the marriage. Since we have been married we have never had a disagreement about money.

In the article "Debt Brought Into Marriage" by James P. Marshall, Ph.D., L.M.F.T. and Linda Skogrand, Ph.D. Family and Human Development Extension Specialists Utah State University, state: "Money is one of the topics couples fight about most often. It is also a contributing factor in divorce. Debt brought into marriage is an especially troublesome part of many couples' money problems. Research shows that debt brought into marriage is the number one problem for newly-weds (Center for Marriage and Family, 2000; Schramm & Lee, 2003).

If you want to become marriage material, get your finances in order first, be like Adam and bring a land marked by abundance to the marriage, don't wait until after you are married to try and create financial stability. Bring something to the table that, as a married couple, you can build on.

"My Babies Need A Daddy"

The number of single parents in our community has grown significantly. According to the U.S. Census Bureau the number of children living with a single parent rose from 5.8 million in 1960 to 19.8 million in 1999. My observation after ministering to single parents is that although they are raising children without a marriage partner, they still have a very strong desire to be married. Some believe marriage will provide their children with the stability and provision of a two-parent home. Theoretically that reasoning is correct. But practically speaking there are flaws in that thinking. There is no guarantee that marriage will produce a stable home for your children. In fact, marriage may produce a more difficult environment for your child if the foundation is not correct. Many children in what is now called "blended homes" suffer physically and emotionally. According to the Stepfamily Foundation, two out of three blended relationships will end in divorce. As I mentioned earlier, my first husband had several children by several different women, and as I endeavored to enter into relationship with them I found it extremely difficult to do with all his children but one. I could not say I loved and cared for them as my own because I did not have children of my own; I had no point of reference. Most of the time I found myself feeling like they were an intrusion to the relationship I wanted to have with their father. To make matters worst, I could not have a relationship with his children that did not also include dealing with their mothers. The mothers of the children were an ongoing reminder to me of the many women my first husband had been intimate with.

Many times when I became angry at his behavior I wanted to take it out on his children. I will never forget one specific incident when my behavior became disgusting toward his children. He went out for the evening and promised to return at a certain time. Several hours passed beyond the promised time before he arrived home. I was furious. I was angry that he had not kept his promise to me and in response to my anger and to get even with him for breaking his promise to me I said to him: "Why did you bother to have a child you did not want (referring to his oldest daughter), you should have just aborted her." This statement infuriated him and deeply wounded our marriage.

I was single until I was 28, and so I had become quite adept at being selfish. Sharing was extremely challenging for me. Many times I was irritable, touchy and resentful with his children. Although I never took the time to ask, I can only imagine that my behavior did not enhance his children's emotional stability. I believe my struggles with stepparenting were not unique to most stepparents and so it is unwise for single parents to believe that marriage will automatically create a better life for their children.

Single parents need to focus on what God promised in His Word: "God saves the fatherless and the poor from the grasp of these oppressors" (Job 5:15, TLB). "Because I delivered the poor who cried out, The fatherless and *the one who* had no helper" (Job 29:12, NKJV). God did not indicate that marriage was the way he was going to keep these promises. If you are a single parent you need to realize that God has a greater concern for your child than you do and is committed to your child's success. He does not need you to plan a marriage that He has not endorsed or prepared you for in order to take care of your children. Trust God—not your marriage plans—to successfully raise your children.

Chapter Three

My Biological Clock Is Ticking!

Single women who desire to have children become very concerned about their ability to get pregnant as they get older. Older women may be at increased risk for miscarriage, birth defects, and pregnancy complications. This creates desire and pressure to get married. Anytime you are pressured into getting married instead of being led by God into a marriage you increase the likelihood of a troubled marriage. The pressure causes you to ignore, excuse or deny the potential problems that exist in a relationship.

As I shared in my story in chapter one, from the time I was a small child I had a desire to get married and have children. I am now 51 years old, and although I am finally a very happily married woman, I have never given birth to a child of my own. When I was 21, unsaved, sexually promiscuous, and selfish, I became pregnant, for the first and only time: I chose to abort the baby. During my first marriage, I refused to get pregnant because the marriage was so troubled I could not see complicating it by adding children to the equation. After the divorce, I never met anyone during those years when physically I may have still been able to get pregnant. When Julius and I married we agreed that we are too old to have children of our own. Instead, we agreed that God had called us to impact His Kingdom by developing *spiritual children*. Julius has three adult children that he has successfully raised to serve the Lord. So, barring God overriding my age and our desire, I will never physically give birth to children.

How did I come to grips with the fact that I will never have children of my own? Several things happened. First, I recognized that my decision to marry the first time—which was based on insecurity, anxiety, low self-esteem and lust—actually deprived me of the opportunity to take advantage of my childbearing years and have children. When I should have been getting pregnant and raising children I was struggling to survive in a destructive, crisis-oriented marriage. Second, after my divorce, as I began to cultivate a genuine passionate relationship with the Lord, my desire to give birth to children of my own diminished and I began to find significant fulfillment in serving in God's kingdom and having God use my life to impact others. I need to be honest and admit that my desire to have children of my own never completely left, but as my biological clock ticked I was able to put this desire in perspective and trust God's guidance in my life, recognizing that my desire was not necessarily God's will at this stage in my life. God helped me work through this difficult loss by becoming to me what children would have been. My relationship with God and serving in his Kingdom primarily through my local church and then starting Singles Pleasing The Lord provided me with the fulfillment I expected children to bring me. This proved to me the place of genuine fulfillment comes from being in the center of God's will and not necessarily from getting married, getting pregnant and raising kids.

If it is God's will for you to have children, and if you walk in obedience, He will make sure you have that opportunity. He is more committed to you experiencing His will for your life than you are. Your responsibility is to not succumb to pressure and take matters into your own hands, but to trust and obey God.

If you are a single adult woman reading this book right now and you have a very strong desire to have children but you have passed the childbearing age, God knows that and He has any number of ways to address that unmet need if you are open and led by the Holy Spirit. A single woman who serves on the Board of Directors of Singles Pleasing The Lord shared with me that she had an ongoing desire to have children, and this desire stayed with her even after she passed the childbearing age. She said God made her a promise from Psalm 113:9: "He makes the barren woman to be a homemaker and a joyful mother of [spiritual] children. Praise the Lord! (Hallelujah!)" She held onto that promise. As a result of her trust in God's promise she is now raising three children. A tragic situation of child neglect and abuse in her family brought these children into her life, but God used that as the occasion to make good on the promise He made her. She is raising these children as if they were her own, and they are growing and thriving. Her home is happy, her joy is full and God's grace is equipping her to be a successful single parent. Unlike many single-parent homes that started as a result of disobedience, not only does she have emotional joy and fulfillment but she also has financial provision and resources readily available to her. She waited on God to make good on his promise, and He was faithful. She did not use her desire to have children to orchestrate a marriage outside God's will.

In chapter one I shared with you my experience with step-parenting and indicated that it was basically a very negative experience with all my first husband's children but one. From the very beginning of the marriage, one of his son's came to live with us. He was eleven at the time, and almost immediately I fell in love with this child. He was charming,

sociable and a delight to be around. He also took an immediate liking to me. I became very involved in parenting him,
helping him with his homework, sometimes conned into
doing it for him, getting him involved in activities at school
and church, watching over his friends, participating in his
disciplining, praying for him, doing all the things that my
limited understanding of parenting at the time indicated I
should do. We became very close. When the marriage began
to openly fail, this son, who by now had emotionally become
my son, chose to cleave to me. When I made the decision to
leave my husband, I shared this with my stepson, and gave
him the option of staying with his dad or returning to his
mother. Much to my surprise like Ruth cleaved to Naomi,
this child who was now one month shy of being 18 cleaved
to me and said, "I want to go with you, please take me with
you." Unsure if it was the right thing to do, I prayed and
decided that he was almost grown and if he wanted to come
with me, he could. We moved out together and I started the
challenging journey of single parenting. During the first few
months of marital separation, when I was depressed, despon-
dent and suicidal, God used this teenager as a lifeline. He
gave me a reason to live. I couldn't give up, because he
needed me to be there for him. He had his own pain with
the marital separation and divorce and began to experience
behavioral problems, such as poor grades and sexual promiscuity. God gave me the grace to endure these, taught me the
power of prayer and fasting for your children and ultimately
allowed me to see him become a man of God in his own
right. He has been married for more than ten years. He has a
growing career, a godly wife and two daughters. He honors
me publicly as the mother who raised him, his wife treats me
life a real mother-in-law (we have a great relationship), and
his daughters treat me like a real grandmother. They have
given me the name "Granny D," and they love to visit. The
whole family also loves Julius and his children, and we enjoy

spending time together as a family. I share this with you, to prove the point that I never had children of my own, but God remembered that childhood desire to have children and took my mistakes and turned them into blessings for me. Out of a troubled marriage and devastating divorce, God salvaged for me a son, daughter-in-law and two granddaughters.

God makes an awesome promise to single adults who pass childbearing age and have not gotten married. Isaiah 54:1-3 says,

Sing, O barren one, you who did not bear; break forth into singing and cry aloud, you who did not travail with child! For the [spiritual] children of the desolate who will be more than the children of the married wife, says the Lord. Enlarge the place of your tent, and let the curtains of your habitations be stretched out; spare not; lengthen your cords and strengthen your stakes, For you will spread abroad to the right hand and to the left; and your offspring will possess the nations and make the desolate cities to be inhabited.

God is promising to single adults who will receive these verses that you can actually have a life that brings greater fulfillment and productivity than the life of a married person, and these verses tell you how to begin to experience it. By praising God for his goodness and his ability to bring meaning to your life without a husband and children and by preparing to experience growth in your ability to have impact on the Kingdom of God. You must expand your vision, cultivate your gifts, watch for open doors and expect God to bring you fulfillment beyond the most happily married person you know. If you permit yourself to be open to these passages instead of believing you are doomed to a life of misery you can forever change your destiny and open the way for God to bring the fulfillment into your life that He wants.

Let me summarize this chapter by saying that you don't need to use your desire to have children to orchestrate a marriage outside of God's will. Give your desire for children to God and trust Him to bring children into your life in the way He sees fit, or bring you fulfillment greater than getting married and having children could ever bring. God is not in the business of disappointing you but blessing you!

Chapter Four

What God Had In Mind When He Created Marriage

N ow that we have looked at all the wrong reasons to get married, I want to focus on how you become marriage material so that you can discover how to receive God's best in a marriage partner and a marriage.

One of the major reasons my first marriage failed is because, although I had a desire for marriage, I had no understanding and appreciation of why God created marriage. I viewed marriage from a totally selfish viewpoint. I looked at marriage in terms of what was in it for me instead of the purpose God had in creating marriage. You can never consider yourself a candidate for a successful marriage if you don't first understand God's foundational purpose for marriage. I did not say you could not get married. Jesus said,

> So everyone who hears these words of Mine and acts upon them [obeying them] will be like a sensible (prudent, practical, wise) man who built his house upon the rock. And the rain fell and the floods came and the winds blew and beat against that house; yet it did not fall, because it had been founded on the

rock. And everyone who hears these words of Mine and does not do them will be like a stupid (foolish) man who built his house upon the sand. And the rain fell and the floods came and the winds blew and beat against that house, and it fell—and great and complete was the fall of it (Matthew 7:24-27).

Many people have entered marriage clueless as to what God had in mind when He created the institution. Consequently, they struggle and fail because their marriage was built on sand. They made the decision to marry on the insufficient foundation of desire.

The foundation for a successful marriage is a clear understanding of God's purpose for marriage as revealed in the Bible. As you examine the following scriptures, ask the Holy Spirit to show you what God really had in mind when He created the institution of marriage. Then trust him to give you the grace to accurately apply the revelation. Genesis 2:18-24 reveals the rock that marriage should be built on.

Now the Lord God said, It is not good (sufficient, satisfactory) that the man should be alone; I will make him a helper meet (suitable, adapted, complementary) for him. And out of the ground the Lord God formed every [wild] beast and living creature of the field and every bird of the air and brought them to Adam to see what he would call them; and whatever Adam called every living creature, that was its name. And Adam gave names to all the livestock and to the birds of the air and to every [wild] beast of the field; but for Adam there was not found a helper meet (suitable, adapted, complementary) for him. And the Lord God caused a deep sleep to fall upon Adam; and while he slept, He took one of his ribs or a part of his side and closed up the [place with] flesh. And the rib or part of his side which the Lord God had taken from the man He built up and made into a woman, and He brought her to the man. Then Adam said, This [creature] is now bone of my bones and flesh of my flesh; she shall be called Woman, because she was taken out of a man. Therefore a man shall leave his father and his mother and shall become united and cleave to his wife, and they shall become one flesh.

From these passages we can see the process God chose to bring about the institution of marriage. First, the idea for Adam to have a helper was God's idea. Adam didn't ask God for companionship. God evaluated Adam's state and decided that it was not good for Adam to be alone. Second, we can see that God formed Adam and Eve, and then He brought Eve to Adam. Adam and Eve were not wandering around aimlessly filled with anxiety and frustration, searching for one another. Adam and Eve were unmarried adults, fashioned by God and trusting Him for His direction for their life. These scripture passages also establish that it was a man and a woman who were joined together as one flesh in marriage, and that the union of a husband and a wife was lifelong.

The Apostle Paul, who was unmarried, provided instructions to married couples that identify the purpose of marriage. In Ephesians 5:22-33 Paul explains why God brought Adam and Eve together in marriage:

Wives, be subject (be submissive and adapt yourselves) to your own husbands as [a service] to the Lord. For the husband is head of the wife as Christ is the Head of the church, Himself the Savior of [His] body. As the church is subject to Christ, so let wives also be subject in everything to their husbands. Husbands, love your wives, as Christ loved the church and gave Himself up for her, So that He might sanc-

tify her, having cleansed her by the washing of water
with the Word, That He might present the church to
Himself in glorious splendor, without spot or wrinkle
or any such things [that she might be holy and fault-
less]. Even so husbands should love their wives as
[being in a sense] their own bodies. He who loves his
own wife loves himself. For no man ever hated his
own flesh, but nourishes and carefully protects and
cherishes it, as Christ does the church, Because we
are members (parts) of His body. **For this reason** a
man shall leave his father and his mother and shall be
joined to his wife, and the two shall become one flesh.
This mystery is very great, but I speak concerning
[the relation of] Christ and the church. However, let
each man of you [without exception] love his wife as
[being in a sense] his very own self; and let the wife
see that she respects and reverences her husband that
she notices him, regards him, honors him, prefers
him, venerates, and esteems him; and that she defers
to him, praises him, and loves and admires him
exceedingly]. (Emphasis added)

These passages describe how the husband and wife are
to relate to one another. The wife is to submit to her husband
and be subject to her husband in the same manner as the
church is subject to Christ. She is to respect her husband
and give her husband the right to give overall guidance and
direction to the marriage. The husband is to love his wife
in the same manner as Christ loves the church, with sacri-
ficial, selfless love and undivided devotion. Verse 31 then
says, "For this reason." *For what reason?* To demonstrate
the relationship that Christ and the church have toward one
another. When two adults come together in marriage, their
greatest desire, goal and aim should be to demonstrate the
relationship Christ and the church share. If this is not your

ultimate goal when you are planning to get married, then your marriage is not being formed on the correct foundation. If you happen to be married and reading this book and that is not the foundation you started your marriage with, it is never too late. As I shared in chapter one, when I married the first time I did it because I was looking for my husband to fill all the voids in my life. I was lonely; I wanted to have sex and not feel guilty; I wanted someone to spend evenings, weekends and holidays with. Even though I knew Ephesians 5:22-33, I did not understand how it applied to my desire for marriage.

I did not enter my marriage with the goal of demonstrating the relationship that Christ and the church share. I did not understand the purpose of marriage, so I could not carry out my God-given responsibility. I struggled to show my first husband respect (the number-one responsibility of a wife in marriage) because I did not know the church demonstrates her love to Christ through reverent willing obedience and submission. I belittled my spouse when he did not treat me the way I felt I deserve to be treated. I nagged him to get my way; I held grudges and brought up old offenses regularly. None of these behaviors describe the way the church is to love Christ. Had I understood how Christ and the Church are to interact, I could have done my part to keep our marriage together instead of helping to destroy it. Had I been diligent in cultivating an intimate close relationship with Christ while I was single (I will talk more about this in a later chapter) I would have developed the ability to successfully interact with my husband. My first marriage was built on sand, and when the storms came it was devastated.

The other purpose for marriage is found in Genesis 1:28a: "And God blessed them, and God said to them, 'Be fruitful and multiply; ...'" To be fruitful and multiply, Adam and Eve needed to be married. So another purpose for marriage is to carry out the assignment God gave mankind to reproduce offspring. This assignment related not only to having babies but also to other productivity that enhances God's Kingdom and manifests His glory. God has designed a specific purpose for every marriage and delegated to every couple specific responsibilities for His kingdom. Maybe God has planned a marriage with a ministry or a marriage with a business for you to direct or manage. As a married couple understands their purpose and carries it out, the Kingdom of God is positively impacted and the goodness of God is demonstrated to others. If your desires for marriage have only focused on what is in it for you and not what is in it for God, then you have missed a primary purpose of marriage. Clearly, Genesis 1:28 reveals God created marriage for what was in it for HIM!

God established marriage as an example of the relationship that Christ and the church are to share, to ensure the reproduction of Godly offspring, and to expand his Kingdom and manifest His glory on earth. When God released me to believe Him for a husband the second time, and I received this revelation from the Scripture, I began to confess that one day I would have a marriage that glorifies God on earth. At my wedding to Julius, many people glorified God for what He had done by bringing us together, acknowledging that only God could have done this. Since I have been remarried I have seen God increase the impact I am having on His Kingdom by causing a greater number of single adults to trust God more intensely and pursue holiness with a greater passion.

Understanding God's plan for marriage is foundational to assessing your readiness for marriage. If you don't know what God wants to happen with your marriage you are not ready to be married. On the other hand, if the Holy Spirit has taught you God's plan for marriage, then you have begun to lay the foundation for becoming marriage material.

I developed my viewpoint regarding marriage the first time from television, from my own selfish desires, and from what I observed from friends and family. Television depicted marriage as this institution that makes all your dreams come true. All the love stories I watched showed a lonely person who met someone and suddenly all their troubles ended. I was always taught that getting married was God's answer to the awful problem of singleness, and if you could just meet someone and get married the miserable single life would suddenly be over and life could finally begin. Before God sent me Julius to marry, I had to undergo a radical mental transformation about marriage. I had to bathe my thoughts in God's Word until I received a God-given, Holy Spirit inspired revelation about God's purpose for marriage. God had to teach me that he created marriage to demonstrate the relationship that Christ and the church have to one another and not to give me someone to take away my loneliness, fill my voids and provide me with a sexual partner. Romans 12:2 says,

> Do not be conformed to this world (this age), [fashioned after and adapted to its external, superficial customs], but be transformed (changed) by the [entire] renewal of your mind [by its new ideals and its new attitude], so that you may prove [for yourselves] what is the good and acceptable and perfect will of God, even the thing which is good and acceptable and perfect [in His sight for you].

In other words, if we want to experience God's will for our life as it relates to marriage then we must begin to transform our thinking so we think what His Word says about marriage. When we think the way God thinks about marriage, then we are on our way to becoming marriage material. Once you know God's reason for creating the institution of marriage, your motivation for wanting to get married can be purified. You can want marriage for the reason God wants to bless you with it.

Chapter Five

Is Your Single Life Successful?

A nother foundational prerequisite for becoming marriage material is living the successful single life. The successful single life prepares you for a successful marriage. Once again, if we go back to the book of Genesis we can see that it was a successful Adam that was led to Eve. Genesis 2:7 reveals the first two indicators of the successful single life. "Then the Lord God formed man from the dust of the ground and breathed into his nostrils the breath or spirit of life, and man became a living being." God first formed Adam. The word *formed* means He shaped and molded Adam and pre-arranged and pre-determined his life. After that, God breathed life into Adam. If I am 1000 feet away and breathe on someone, I am too far away for my breath to have impact on that person. The closer I get and breathe the greater impact my breath will have. The person I am breathing on will be able to feel and experience my breath. In order for Adam to have impact from God's breath he had to be close to God. God's breath gave this single adult life. Before God breathed on Adam he was dead. Adam had a life that had been pre-arranged by God, but he could not experience it because God had not breathed on him and empowered him to live successfully. The passage says Adam became a living being. According to the Old Testament Hebrew Lexicon, definitions given to the words "living being" include "to live," "have life," "remain alive," "sustain life," "live prosperously," "live forever," "be quickened," "be alive," "be restored to life or health." When God breathed life into Adam, He breathed into him the ability to live a prosperous and a purposeful life. The lexicon goes on to describe this life as being free from sickness, discouragement, faintness and death. Adam was very close to God to get the full impact of God's breath. Single adults who want to live successfully must choose to be formed by God, which means they must realize and accept God's pre-arranged plan for their lives and then they must develop a very close relationship with God so that He can breathe on them and empower them for success. Without this intimate contact, single adults are incapable of living a successful single life.

Singles who develop a very close relationship with God are also able to bring the benefit of that intimacy into their marriage. They have learned to be submissive to God and His Word, and this submissive attitude is vitally important for a successful marriage. If you are first submitted to God, it is much easier to submit to another person. Whenever Julius and I have a conflict we immediately ask what God's Word says about the situation and then, rather than argue, we agree to line ourselves up with the Word. My flesh does not always like this, but learning to be submissive to God and his Word while I was single prepared me for marital submission.

Also, Julius is extremely romantic and understands how to be intimate with me. He will bring me one rose sometimes, and sometimes he will bring me a dozen. Sometimes he writes me a love note and places it on my mirror so that when I come out of the shower it will surprise me. Sometimes he will buy my favorite treat or just hold me close and whisper he loves me. All these are gestures of intimacy that he is quite skilled at, and they cause my love for him to grow. I am convinced that as he cultivated his very close relationship with the Lord he learned the basic principles of intimacy, how to be attentive and responsive to the needs of his first Lover the Lord and now he successfully applies them to marriage.

Genesis 2:8-14 then reveals the next indicator of the successful single life.

And the Lord God planted a garden toward the east in Eden [delight]; and there He put the man whom He had formed, (framed and constituted). And out of the ground the Lord God made to grow every tree that is pleasant to the sight or to be desired-good (suitable, pleasant) for food; the tree of the knowledge of [the difference between] good and evil and blessing and calamity. Now a river went out of Eden to water the garden and from there it divided and became four [river] heads. The first is named Pishon; it is the one around the whole land of Havilah, where there is gold. The gold of that land is of high quality; bdelellium (pearl?) and onyx stone are there. The second river is Gihon; it is the one flowing around the whole land of Cush. The third river is named Hiddekel [the Tigris]; it is the one flowing east of Assyria. And the fourth river is the Euphrates.

After Adam was formed and intimate with God, God made and placed Adam in a land marked by abundance. Adam received God's provision. Successful singles walk close enough to God that they are led to His source to get their temporal needs met. Financial lack and mismanagement are indicators that the single life is not being lived out successfully and is more than likely tied to a lack of intimacy with God because God led Adam to the Garden of Eden after he formed him and breathed on him.

The next indicator of the successful single life is found in Genesis 2:19-20a:

> And out of the ground the Lord God formed every [wild] beast and living creature of the field and every bird of the air and brought them to Adam to see what he would call them; and whatever Adam called every living creature, that was its name. And Adam gave names to all the livestock and to the birds of the air and to every [wild] beast of the field.

God revealed to Adam his assignment in the Kingdom, and because God had breathed on Adam and they were in an ongoing intimate relationship, Adam was very successful at this assignment. Adam named every animal God created. Adam experienced success and fulfillment in the assignment God gave him. He was a complete individual.

In summary successful single living is marked by the following:

- Discovery of God's pre-arranged and pre-determined path for your life — working with creation
- Empowerment to live that life through ongoing intimate contact with God
- Discovery and placement in God's place of provision to meet your temporal needs
- Discovery and implementation of your kingdom assignment marked by success and fulfillment

To this successful single, God said: "Now the Lord God said, It is not good (sufficient, satisfactory) that the man should be alone; I will make him a helper meet (suitable, adapted, complementary) for him" (Gen. 2:18). Adam's success as a single prepared him to receive God's helper, his own marriage partner formed and sent by God.

Before God brought me to Julius, I became a successful single. As I grew in my intimacy with God, God formed me into a woman of God who had a passionate, vibrant, intimate relationship with Him, a woman who had her bills paid and who was operating in the Kingdom of God, effectively experiencing a tremendous amount of fulfillment. While Julius and I were dating and preparing for marriage he made a statement to me that proved he was successful at being single after his wife died. He told me, "I have no voids that God has not filled. I am not interested in you to fill voids and address unmet needs in my life." Julius did not need me to bring him money, sex or fulfillment. We knew God was bringing us together to show the relationship Christ and the church have to one another, and to accomplish God's will for our lives as a couple.

Marriage has its own unique satisfaction and joy. I am thoroughly enjoying married life, but I am convinced that experiencing a successful single life was the necessary prerequisite for my current happiness. If you desire to become marriage material, discover and apply the principles of successful single living. They set the stage for you to receive God's best!

Chapter Six

"God Said He Would Give Me the Desires of My Heart"

How many times have you said, "I have a desire to be married and God said He would give me the desires of my heart." There is an element of truth to that statement, but it can also be very misleading without an adequate understanding of the Bible. Psalms 37:4 says, "Delight yourself also in the Lord, and He will give you the desires and secret petitions of your heart." Most of us zero in on the second half of this passage with little or no regard for the first half. Examining the entire verse, however, makes it apparent that to receive the desires of your heart you must first delight yourself in the Lord. Delighting yourself in the Lord ensures that your desires are molded into God's desires. When your desires are one with God's, then whatever you desire will be granted. In order for your desires to be one with God's desires you must delight yourself in Him.

What does it mean to delight yourself in the Lord? According to the Old Testament Hebrew Lexicon, the Hebrew word for delight is "anag," which means "to be soft, delicate or pliable." A person who is soft or pliable is also flexible, adaptable; yielding easily to others. When you

delight yourself in the Lord, you make yourself totally available to Him and yield to His way and not your own. You
adapt your thoughts and actions to line up with His thoughts
and desires for your life. You become interested in knowing
and implementing His agenda, rather than your own. God's
wish, whatever it might be, becomes your command. If He
tells you to discontinue a relationship, then you are soft,
pliable and obedient—you obey. If He tells you to get up
a half and hour earlier so you can spend more time in His
Word and in prayer, then you are flexible and adapt your
sleeping habits to meet His request. If He tells you to fast
and pray to gain control over your sexual drive, you adapt
your eating habits and prayer time to meet His request. As
you delight yourself in the Lord, He molds your desires into
His will and then He grants you your desires.

Many people think Psalm 37:4 means God will give
us whatever we want, if we want it bad enough. But God's
Word does not say that just because you want a marriage
partner—no matter how intense your desire—He is going
to give you a marriage partner. God is quite focused and, in
fact, God is actually quite egocentric. God is concerned with
the implementation of His will, His purposes and His plan.
God is interested in accomplishing His agenda, His vision
and His mission, and to the extent you are interested in that,
you can be assured that God is interested in granting your
desires. 1 John 5:14 says, "And this is the confidence (the
assurance, the privilege of boldness) which we have in Him:
[we are sure] that if we ask anything (make any request)
according to His will (in agreement with His own plan), He
listens to and hears us."

When our desires are one with God's desires, then and
only then will God give us the desires of our heart.

How do we align our desires with God? In order for our
desires to become one with the Lord, we must be in right
relationship with Him. Jesus Christ must be our Savior and

our Lord. When Jesus is your Savior, you believe and trust that His death on the cross has taken care of sin's penalty for you personally. When Jesus is Lord, you give Him permission to direct every aspect of your life. According to *Strong's Concordance* the Hebrew word for lord is "adon," which means "owner and master." When you decide that Jesus is Lord of your life you are agreeing to totally submit your will to His will. He becomes your personal owner and master. You are not doing this out of bondage or fear like a slave to his master, but willfully, with joy and peace, knowing that this is the key to successful living. The intensive form of "adon" is Adonai, and it means "glorious Lord in all His powers and attributes." When you understand and appreciate His glorious powers and attributes you willingly give him ownership of your life and permission to direct your life.

When Jesus is permitted to operate in the position of Lord in our life, then our aim and goal in life is to please Him. Operating with Jesus as our Lord is an evolving process. As we grow in our relationship with Him, it is easier to let Him be Lord. The more we understand His character attributes and His method of operation, the more we count it a privilege and an opportunity for Him to be Lord. As the old gospel hymn says, "Can't Nobody Do Me Like Jesus!" After my first marriage failed, I made a major relationship change with Jesus; I expanded His ability to have impact on my life by permitting him to not only be Savior but also my Lord. My pain caused me say to Him, "Lord I don't know how to run my life. Look at the mess I am in, please help me." That simple appeal with a genuine heart caused God's role in my life and impact on my life to change. I began to consult God about matters that I used to act independently on, such as dating, how I spent my time, what I did with my money and what activities I would get involved in. His input coupled with my obedience made a phenomenal change in my life.

I began to experience the single life He wanted me to have all along.

The greater the degree of intimacy we cultivate with the Lord, the more we will give Him permission to direct every aspect of our life. When He is operating as Lord, your desire for a marriage partner becomes His choice and not your need. You give Him permission to choose whether He wants you to be married and who your marriage partner is going to be. You give him permission to select the time and location. You don't say, "God, I am lonely, send me someone to marry," or "God I want to have sex, send me a marriage partner." What you do say is, "God I belong to you; do with my life according to your perfect plan and I will trust you." You are only able to relinquish this decision-making to God when you are intimate enough with Him and His character to trust Him to do what's best for you. God does not want to withhold a marriage partner from you. He wants to protect you from the wrong relationships, the devastation of divorce and missed opportunities and blessings that come when you miss His will for your life.

Giving Jesus Lordship over your life does not mean He will take away your desire for marriage. It means He will mold you to become the person He needs you to be so that you can marry the person He wants you to marry and have the type of marriage He wants you to have. Proverbs 16:3 says it this way: "Roll your works upon the Lord [commit and trust them wholly to Him; He will cause your thoughts to become agreeable to His will, and] and so shall your plans be established and succeed." When you are able to say, "God I trust you to do what is best for me regarding marriage; I give my desire to you; do what you know is best for me," then you are committing your desire to the Lord because you trust Him. This Proverbs 16:3 passage says that when you genuinely commit your desire to the Lord and trust Him, your thoughts and desires become agreeable to His will and then He will permit your plans—including those regarding marriage—to be established and succeed.

Those who are led by a desire for marriage, without Jesus as Lord of their life, will miss the opportunity to have His involvement in the selection of their lifetime companion. They also miss the marriage preparation He wants to provide, and the pre-marriage accomplishments and blessings He wants to give them. Many single adults destroy the blessings and accomplishments God pre-arranged for their single life by being too marriage focused. I know marriage in the will of the Lord is very fulfilling. Marriage can bring happiness and satisfaction to your life. But I have come to realize that God wants to bring equal happiness, satisfaction and fulfill-ment to you while you are single. It would go against God's character to call you to live a single life until you are 35 or even 50 and have your single life be less fulfilling than a couple that has been married fifteen years. John 10:10b says, "I came that they may have and enjoy life, and have it in abundance (to the full, till it overflows)." That scripture applies to married and single people equally.

When Jesus is Lord, you are able to release your desire for marriage to Him and say, "Lord not my will, but Your will be done." This submission will keep you from orches-trating your own marriage motivated by lust, loneliness or lack. By submitting, you allow the Holy Spirit to direct your experiences in order to prepare you to be a spouse. He may have you work in the nursery or teach in the Sunday school to prepare you for parenting responsibilities. He may have you travel for your employer in order to make extra income so your wife will not have to work, or go on a missions trip in order to learn how to be a missionary, because He plans for you to marry a missionary. Or He may have you develop a prayer life that He will use to prepare you to be the first-lady of a church. You benefit from God's wisdom about His plans for you when you let Him become Lord.

I am convinced that during my second season of single-ness God was preparing me to be the wife I am today. I learned how to organize and run a successful children's ministry, lead a power packed-prayer meeting, raise a signif-icant offering and endure the pain and challenges of starting a ministry. All these experiences are proving extremely valu-able for me as a wife and helper to Julius. Not only was God preparing me for remarriage, being involved in these activities also brought me a tremendous amount of fulfill-ment while single.

There are varying degrees of desire. A desire can be clas-sified as a wish, a want or something you crave or covet. A wish is a vague or passing longing; a want implies a felt need or lack; crave suggests strongly the force of physical appetite or emotional need; and covet implies a strong eager desire, often inordinate and envious and often for what belongs to another. When the desire for a marriage partner is not submitted to God's will it can very easily progress through these degrees and become dangerous.

As my story reveals, people who crave and covet marriage will do almost anything to get married, including entering into compromise with Biblical standards. They will commit sexual sin, enter into unequally yoked relationships, date married people and spend unwisely to attract or buy the attention of a potential marriage partner. This unfulfilled desire will lead to depression, despair and despondency. When you permit your desire to become so intense that you want it more than you want God, that desire becomes an idol. This idol-like desire will control and direct your life. Those who marry with a covetous desire can't expect God's blessing to be upon their union. In fact the scripture strongly warns us to stay away from idolatry and wanting anything more than we want God.

Therefore, my dearly beloved, shun (keep clear away from, avoid by flight if need be) any sort of idolatry (of loving or venerating anything more than God). (1 Corinthians 10:14)

Giving your desire to God and trusting Him to fulfill your life and provide you with a marriage partner—if that is what He has prearranged for your life—will prevent your desire from turning into a craving or covetousness. God has a predetermined will for every person's life; a will that is marked by fulfillment and success. And He will make sure that those who allow Him to direct their path will discover it. You must not be driven by your desire. Proverbs 3:5-6 says, "Lean on, trust in, and be confident in the Lord with all your heart and mind and do not rely on your own insight or understanding. In all your ways know, recognize, and acknowledge Him, and He will direct and make straight and plain your paths."

How did I get rid of my craving and covetous desire for marriage? It wasn't easy. It required a Gethsemane experience of my marriage desire and a transformation by the Word of God. After my first marriage ended, my answer to the disgust I had for the single life was to just get married again. I had no desire to discover God's purpose and fulfillment *through* the single life. To fix my singleness problem I began to ask God to give me a man to marry—this time a good one. His response was to eliminate all prospects. I had never had a problem landing a date when I was single the first time. As I shared with you in an earlier chapter I could meet a man anyplace; at the store, while driving in the car, anywhere! After my divorce, my appearance improved. I looked better than I did when I was married, or even before I was married. I lost 10 pounds and my hair grew, which made me much more attractive. I shouldn't have had trouble getting a date, but I did. I asked God about this, and then I began to realize that He had, in a sense, put a wall around me to protect me for His purposes. So instead of resisting it, I yielded to it; instead of taking the situation into my own hands and getting what I wanted—a man and a marriage—I went along with God. I surrendered my desire and will to God.

Even so, my desire to get married dominated my thought life. I was growing spiritually, and God was beginning to use me in ministry. However, secretly, I still wanted to be married more than I wanted anything else. During this time I developed some strong mental and emotional attachments to a couple of men who had no idea I was interested in them. I was very disappointed as I watched them get married. I began to pray and fast about God's will for my life. Secretly, I think I believed that if I fasted and prayed God would be impressed and give me what I wanted—a new husband. Quite the opposite happened, during this fast God gave me the direction that began to turn my single state from a problem to a gift. In a book that I was reading during this time I learned about the importance of wanting God more than anything else. Because I was fasting, I was extremely sensitive to the Holy Spirit, and I felt a strong conviction that I still wanted a husband more than I wanted God. The book I was reading instructed me to write my greatest desire on a piece of paper and take a match and burn the paper. This would serve as a symbolic reminder that the desire had been taken off the throne of my life and that it no longer had first place in my life. I wrote my desire for marriage and the two men I had allowed myself to develop secret emotional attachments to on the paper and lit the paper. The match immediately burned out and only a very small amount of the paper was burned. I struck another match and lit the paper and once again only a small amount of the paper burned, and the match went out. The paper was not wet and the matches were not defective, but it took an entire book of matches to burn one sheet of paper. I knew then that God was using this experience to let me know how deeply embedded and strong my desire for marriage was. My desire for marriage was an idol, and God was seeking to destroy that idol once and for all.

Also during this fast the Lord led me to a scripture that let me know that, at least for that season in my life, He was not planning marriage for me. The scripture was 2 Corinthians 11:2: "I am jealous for you with a godly jealousy. I promised you to one husband, to Christ, so that I might present you as a pure virgin to him" (NIV). I tried to resist this scripture because it was not what I wanted to hear from God. In fact, when I first read the scripture I rebuked the devil for speaking a lie to me. As I continued to ponder this scripture I wept and felt deep anguishing pain because I knew that God was asking me to give up the one desire that meant more to me than anything, even God. This scripture was not what I was looking for God to tell me during this fast, but ultimately I made the decision to yield to His direction through His Word. *Over time*, I was able to discover fulfillment, satisfaction and fruitfulness with my single life. I began to want God and His will more than I wanted anything else. I now understand the wisdom of God in requiring me to take my marriage desire to Gethsemane.

Until I was willing to give up the desire for marriage— not knowing whether I would ever be able to remarry and say to the Lord not my will, but your will be done—the desire remained my idol. But once I released the desire, I gave God the opportunity to become the center of my joy and the focus of my attention. Then I was ready to handle the desire without it having and controlling me. You will never qualify to become marriage material until your desire for marriage is on the altar and it doesn't matter whether you get married or not as long as you are in the center of God's will. When you get to that place—and it's a process—then you are ready. Sometimes the desire must die daily until it is completely dead. You do this by not permitting your thoughts and actions about marriage to dominate you, but by deliberately giving them to God every time they try to rule in your life. This is not easy, but it is necessary if you're ever going to become marriage material.

Chapter 7

Lifelong Singles

Not every single adult is going to get married and so I believe that it is very important for us to talk about this. God calls some to remain single lifelong. Matthew 19:10-11 says, "The disciples said to Him, If the case of a man with his wife is like this, it is neither profitable nor advisable to marry. But He said to them, Not all men can accept this saying, but it is for those to whom [the capacity to receive] it has been given." After hearing Jesus share that the only time divorce was permissible was in the case of sexual immorality the disciples felt that it might be better not to ever get married, and Jesus then shared that there are some singles who have been given the desire, capacity and the grace to live the unmarried life. So in the will of the Lord there are some single adults who will not get married. I think it is also appropriate to mention here that for the length of time that God chooses you to live the single life he gives you the capacity and grace to live it successfully if you live it in obedience to His Word. Realizing this is possible, some of you may be filled with dread and fear that you may be one of those lifelong singles. Please don't respond in fear to the possibility that you might never get married. Instead, respond in faith, being convinced of God's love and plan for your life. As I said earlier, Jesus came for you to live the abundant life, and the criteria for that is not your marital status but your trust in him. Jeremiah 29:11 says: "I have not lost sight of my plan for you, the Lord says, and it is your welfare I have in mind, not your undoing, **for you, too,** I have a destiny and a hope" (Knox Bible, Emphasis added) *For single adults too,* God has planned an abundant and fulfilled life. It will take trust and courage on your part to embrace this promise as a single adult. God has not reserved the single life for misery or punishment.

God's will for Jeremiah was that he remain unmarried. Jeremiah 16:2 says, "You shall not take a wife or have sons and daughters in this place [Jerusalem]." God's will for Anna after her husband died was that she not remarry. Luke 2:36-37 says,

> And there was also a prophetess, Anna, the daughter of Phanuel, of the tribe of Asher. She was very old, having lived with her husband seven years from her maidenhood, And as a widow even for eighty-four years. She did not go out from the temple enclosure, but was worshiping night and day with fasting and prayer.

In 1 Corinthians 7:8 we see that Paul was not married: "But to the unmarried people and to the widows, I declare that it is well (good, advantageous, expedient, and wholesome) for them to remain [single] even as I do." Jeremiah, Paul and Anna remained single, and yet their lives were marked by fulfillment and productivity. Jeremiah was a bold yet compassionate prophet who served as God's mouthpiece to Judah and Jerusalem. God entrusted Jeremiah with wealth in order to accomplish His will in Jeremiah's life. On one occasion God instructed Jeremiah to buy a plot of land, and

Jeremiah had access to the financial resources to accomplish this task without difficulty (see Jeremiah 32:7-9). How many single adults do you know who have enough money available to help their pastor build a new church debt free?

Paul was an apostle and author who wrote a large percentage of the New Testament and had a ministry marked by signs and wonders. As a widow, Anna devoted her life to God who promised to be a Husband to her. Anna had a prayer and worship life as a single woman that gave her the awesome opportunity to reveal the birth of Jesus as the Messiah. Julius has a 43-year-old brother who is a pastor in Nigeria who has never been married. He does not have a desire to be married and wants to devote his life to serving the Lord without distraction. He is fulfilled, satisfied and successful with the single life. If Jesus is Lord of your life, He will let you know as he did these three single adults if He wants you to remain single—and He will bring you fulfillment without a marriage partner. Some single adults need to know this, because the pressure in today's society particularly in the church to get married is very strong. In some cases you are made to feel abnormal if you don't want to get married. Don't conform to the world, but discover God's will and live a fulfilled and successful unmarried life, if that is God's will for you.

Chapter Eight

Have You Dealt With Destiny?

The Word of God teaches us that God has a prearranged and predetermined plan for every person's life. Ephesians 2:10 says,

> For we are God's [own] handiwork (His workmanship), recreated in Christ Jesus, [born anew] that we may do those good works which God predestined (planned beforehand) for us [taking paths which He prepared ahead of time], that we should walk in them [living the good life which He prearranged and made ready for us to live].

A purposeful life is available to you when you are recreated in Christ Jesus. Many people believe that when they get married they will discover God's purpose for their life. I have heard some bachelors say that when they get married they will settle down and make something of their lives, as if being a bachelor excused them from living their life with purpose. They seem to be waiting on marriage to define who they are and what they should be doing with their life. Marriage is not meant to help you determine your purpose.

The discovery of purpose and destiny should begin when you accept Jesus Christ as your Savior and Lord. This does not mean that when you marry your purpose will not be more defined; life is a journey, and God reveals Himself to us as we go and as we grow. But we should not wait until we are married for the revelation to begin.

If you don't know God's individual plan for your life, interaction with a marriage partner will not help you discover it; only interaction with God can bring you purpose, because God is the author of the plan for your life. Although I quoted this scripture in the last chapter it bears repeating here - Jeremiah 29:11: "I know what I'm doing. I have it all planned out—plans to take care of you, not abandon you, plans to give you the future you hope for" (MSG).

God can more easily direct those who understand His plan for their lives. If you are interested in American politics and government, then it's unlikely that God will lead you to someone He has called to overseas missions work. Before Julius and I were married, God gave him a vision for a ministry that included three components: meet the needs of people, grow the Body of Christ, and glorify God's name. Meanwhile, God assigned me to establish and direct the Ministry of Singles Pleasing The Lord in order to prepare single adults to impact God's Kingdom. As my husband and I grow in our oneness, we are starting to see how our ministry visions complement and enhance each other.

When you get married, these details may not all be worked out so that you can appreciate it, but if you are led by the Holy Spirit, He has already worked out the details and will navigate you through the process. Knowing this, your prerequisites for a marriage partner will go beyond a pretty face, a hefty bank account and someone who enjoys sports. You will want to bring more in to your marriage than an active social calendar. You will want to know that your potential marriage partner has discovered God's predetermined plan for their life. You may not know everything about God's gradually unfolding plan for your life. Some parts of your destiny may not be revealed until after you are married, but you should discover something about what God wants you to do with your life and be implementing it with some degree of success and fulfillment while you are single. Maybe God will have you complete a degree, start a business, take missionary trips, experience success in corporate America or be active in your local church.

People who fail to discover God's purpose for their life before they get married run the risk of selecting a person who will not help them meet that purpose. Eve's God-given purpose was to specifically help Adam carry out his God-given purpose. Genesis 2:18 says, "Now the Lord God said, It is not good (sufficient, satisfactory) that the man should be alone; I will make him a helper meet (suitable, adapted, complementary) for him." God gave Adam someone who was suited just for him, someone who complemented him. It will be difficult for a man to provide leadership to a woman when he has no interest or skill in the area God has planned for her life. On the other hand, Julius serves as an excellent leader for me because he is mature in the spiritual disciplines, such as prayer and fasting and studying God's Word. I am detailed-oriented and able to implement plans and goals. My husband is visionary, and able to see the global picture and plan long range. God has prepared my husband to lead me and prepared me to help him.

As I stated earlier, when I was a young, adult single I was very focused on dating and marriage. The majority of conversations I had with God were to tell him to hurry up and send me someone to marry. It never entered my mind that God had something He wanted me to accomplish for His kingdom while I was single. I had no idea He wanted me to preach the gospel, minister to single adults and host radio and television programs. If I had known that I would have started a lot sooner. But God could not tell me about His plan because I was too busy making my own plans. But thank God after the devastating impact of divorce on my life God was able to get my attention and now His purposes and plans are prevailing in my life. Proverbs 19:21 says, "Many plans are in a man's mind, but it is the Lord's purpose for him that will stand." In addition, He is now using my mistakes and failures for good. Romans 8:28 says, "We are assured and know that God being a partner in their labor] all things work together and are [fitting into a plan] for good to and for those who love God and are called according to [His] design and purpose."

People who qualify as marriage material have at a very minimum a general idea of the direction God is leading their life, and they are pursuing it aggressively. If you are clueless as to why God created you, I believe your time would be better spent pursuing His will, His purpose and His plan for your life. You're not ready for marriage.

Chapter Nine

"The Closer I Get To You"

One of the best ways to ensure you are marriage material is to cultivate intimacy with the Lord. Adults who spend their single life establishing close relationships with the Lord make the best marriage partners. The closer you get to Jesus, the better marriage partner you become. This is especially true for men because they are to love women as Jesus loves the church. What better way to find out how Jesus does that then to get to know Jesus well so He can show you. I shared with you in an earlier chapter that I am convinced that one of the reasons Julius is so skillful at romancing me is because he is intimate with the Lord. He enjoys worship and time alone in God's presence. He has an incredible prayer life, waking most mornings at 6:00 A.M. to spend quality time with the Lord. Over the years this has taught him intimacy, and I am a very blessed woman today, reaping the benefits of that intimacy.

Have you ever considered that the reason you can't seem to land a date and the relationships you become involved in keep failing is because God wants to be alone with you and develop a closer relationship with you? During one of my seasons of frustration with the single life, to help me calm down and get peace, God said, "Debbie, I want you for myself." I knew then, that at least for that season in my life, God was not interested in sharing me with anyone else. With reluctance I yielded to God's request, and I will be eternally glad that I did. That time with Him forever changed my life and prepared me to become marriage material. Without a doubt I can say I am happily married today because, while I was single, I became intimate with God and not man! My concern is that many single adults miss the greatest opportunity that God gives them to become close to him – their season of singleness. Married people lack the time and the opportunity that single people have to develop closeness to God. The scripture says so in 1 Corinthians 7:33: "But the married man is anxious about worldly matters—how he may please his wife- And he is drawn in diverging directions [his interests are divided and he is distracted from his devotion to God]." I must admit that since I have been married it has been very challenging to find that time for undistracted, undivided devotion to God that I had while single. I thank God I took advantage of the opportunity He gave me for undistracted time with Him during my years of singleness after my divorce.

Intimate relationships are personal; characterized by deep affection and devotion. Intimate relationships are intense and passionate. In order to cultivate intimacy with someone you must spend quality time with that person; you begin to take on that person's characteristics. You begin to think like they think, talk like they talk and do what they do. Unmarried adults who pay the price to become intimate with the Lord make the best lovers in marriage. While cultivating intimacy with Him you will get a deep, abiding revelation of what love is and how to be a lover. What better person to teach you about love, than the author of love. He reveals the magnitude of His love while you are being intimate with Him and then you are able to demonstrate that love to the person He calls you to marry. What better person to teau.. you about sex, than the creator of sex? When you are intimate with the Lord, He will equip you to be intimate with your marriage partner.

How do you develop the level of intimacy that prepares you to be marriage material? Developing intimacy requires giving undistracted, undivided devotion to the person you want to be intimate with. Single adults (particularly those without parenting responsibilities) have the greatest opportunity to develop intimacy. Their time and energies are available to pay the price of developing their relationship with the Lord. Developing intimacy requires a diligent, deliberate, tenacious, persistent pursuit of God.

God is continually inviting unmarried adults to become intimate with Him. Psalms 65:4 says, "Blessed (happy, fortunate, to be envied) is the man whom You choose and cause to come near, that he may dwell in Your courts! We shall be satisfied with the goodness of Your house, Your holy temple." When the Holy Spirit extends the invitation for you to come into His presence, you must accept it. You must free up your schedule and take the time to establish a close relationship with Him. The more you realize how much God loves you, the more you will be driven to pursue intimacy with Him. God demonstrated the massiveness and the extravagance of His love when Jesus died on Calvary's cross. Not only that, God has made His presence so awesome that once you really begin to share intimacy with Him and spend time in His presence, you will not find anything more satisfying and fulfilling, not even spending time with a husband or a wife. Psalms 16:11 says, "You will show me the path of life; in Your presence is fullness of joy, at Your right hand there are pleasures forevermore." Even though I am happily married now, and I love the many intimate moments I have with my husband, I still want, need and look forward to being alone with the Lord!

In order to establish intimacy with God you must understand the rules of intimacy. You must have the right location, a place free of distraction. One of my favorite places to be alone with God is in the shower. I can relax, I can worship and I can hear his voice. There have been times when I have had an intimate moment in the car, kitchen and even the toilet. Some people create a certain area of their home to be alone with God. Before we were married, Julius used a large walk-in closet. You must have the right atmosphere. The Lord loves praise and worship. In fact He is looking for those who will worship Him in Spirit and in truth. You must have the right heart- a heart that is totally devoted to Him, pure and free of deception. It won't help to spend time with Him because you don't have anything better to do and—maybe—then, "You will give me what I really want: a marriage partner." You must understand the art of communication. There must be a time for both people to express themselves, and a time when both people listen to their lover and give feedback. I will let you in on a secret that I have discovered about developing intimacy with God: He enjoys the time spent most with those who don't dominate the conversation, but those who listen and allow Him to respond and give feedback. There is nothing like feedback from the throne room of God.

As you grow in intimacy with the Lord you will discover that your intimate times of fellowship will be marked by uniqueness and individuality. They will be marked by expressions of the love that the two of you have for one another. Your Lover may request a special song or a dance. You may just desire to sit in holy silence in your lover's presence and bask in His peace.

I will never forget the season when God chose me and drew me into His presence for intimacy. It was during the painful healing process of my divorce. I knew I needed to move on with life, but I didn't always feel as if that's what I wanted to do. It was a Saturday evening, and I was driving home alone from a fellowship I had attended with some friends. I was reflecting on the good time I had and dreading the fact that the only thing this Saturday evening held for me was loneliness and pain in my apartment. The Holy Spirit asked me, "Debbie, what if you were going home and waiting for you was someone tall, dark and handsome waiting to take you out on date? Would you want to go home then?" I began to smile from ear to ear as I responded, "Lord, you know I would." Then the Holy Spirit replied," I am waiting." I went home that night and determined to go on a date with God. I created an atmosphere for my new Lover by turning down the lights, lighting my favorite scented candles and playing my favorite praise and worship music. I sat on my loveseat for two and I said, "God I am here for a date with you, what do we do now?" I must admit, at first I felt awkward, but as I made the decision to enjoy myself alone in God's presence, He began to manifest Himself to me. That night was the beginning of my Saturday-night dates with God for the next couple of years, and I am living off the fruit of that intimacy today. God intends for His intimate presence to be the most valuable and fulfilling experience a person can have.

Singles that have discovered the place of God's presence and are in intimate relationship with Him are better off than the happiest married couple on the earth. God would never elevate a happy and successful marriage over the joy of an intimate relationship with Him. You may not be married, but if you are intimate with the Lord, you are not deficient in anyway. Single adults desiring to be married need to discover the place of God's presence and be intimate with Him; this is the best way to prepare to become marriage material and to be totally and completely satisfied while waiting.

Chapter Ten

"The Just Shall Live By Faith"

Successful living in God's Kingdom requires the ability to live by faith. Hebrews 11:6 says, "But without faith it is impossible to please and be satisfactory to Him. For whoever would come near to God must [necessarily] believe that God exists and that He is the rewarder of those who earnestly and diligently seek Him [out]." If God is pleased, He is moved to fulfill His promises in your life. If you are marriage material, in order to receive your mate from God you must use your faith. If you are not marriage material, God will not honor your faith because you don't qualify for the blessing.

As it relates to a marriage partner, faith is your assurance that you have one (a future spouse), even though you may not currently see him or her. Faith says, "I am going to be married to God's choice for me in His time." Faith is not shaken by the lack of available men or women in your local church. Faith hangs on despite the fact that you have not dated in ten years. Faith holds on even when the girl you were sure was God's choice for you just married another guy. Faith gives assurance to the fact that God has a marriage partner for you. My constant confession before marrying

Julius was, "God has a man with my name on him!" I held on to that truth.

Faith for a marriage partner must be developed, just like faith for any of God's promises. Romans 10:17 says, "So then faith *comes* by hearing, and hearing by the word of God." (NKJV) If you are going to develop faith for a marriage partner, then you must hear a word from God. Your desire for a marriage partner must be backed up with a personal promise from God that He has promised you a marriage partner. The promise must be specific word from God spoken personally to you. You can't receive a marriage partner from God if He does not speak to you personally and make you a promise. Having a marriage desire does not necessarily mean God has spoken to you and promised that he has a marriage planned for you. As we shared earlier, desires for marriage can come from loneliness and lust too.

Eight years after my divorce God spoke to me personally about marrying again. I was concluding a time of prayer and fasting that I like to do at the end of the year in preparation for the following year. I decided to ask God if he had any plans for me regarding marriage. To this request I heard only silence and decided to take the silence to mean no. I entered into a time of praise to God and was led to Psalm 45.

> My heart is stirred by a noble theme as I recite my verses for the king; my tongue is the pen of a skillful writer. You are the most excellent of men and your lips have been anointed with grace, since God has blessed you forever. Gird your sword upon your side, O mighty one; clothe yourself with splendor and majesty. In your majesty ride forth victoriously in behalf of truth, humility and righteousness; let your right hand display awesome deeds. Let your sharp arrows pierce the hearts of the king's enemies; let the nations fall beneath your feet. Your throne, O God,

will last for ever and ever; a scepter of justice will be the scepter of your kingdom. You love righteousness and hate wickedness; therefore God, your God, has set you above your companions by anointing you with the oil of joy. All your robes are fragrant with myrrh and aloes and cassia; from palaces adorned with ivory the music of the strings makes you glad. Daughters of kings are among your honored women; at your right hand is the royal bride in gold of Ophir. Listen, O daughter, consider and give ear: Forget your people and your father's house. The king is enthralled by your beauty; honor him, for he is your lord. he Daughter of Tyre will come with a gift, men of wealth will seek your favor. All glorious is the princess within her chamber her gown is interwoven with gold. In embroidered garments she is led to the king her virgin companions follow her and are brought to you. They are led in with joy and gladness; they enter the palace of the king. Your sons will take the place of your fathers; you will make them princes throughout the land. I will perpetuate your memory through all generations; therefore the nations will praise you for ever and ever (Psalm 45, NIV).

Being led to this Psalm, a wedding song that prophetically describes the relationship of Christ and his bride, the church indicated to me that God was speaking to me about future wedding plans. I paid particularly close attention to the dress the bride wore in verse 13. It was interwoven with gold. Remembering this encounter with the Holy Spirit, when it was time for me to purchase my wedding dress, I sought a wedding gown interwoven with gold, and the Holy Spirit led me to the perfect one. To confirm that I had God's choice, God also showed it to my husband. Shortly after I purchased my dress, my then fiancé, who is known for having accurate visions, shared with me that God had shown him my wedding gown, and I looked beautiful. Stunned by this, and knowing what God had promised me and also the wedding gown I had just purchased, I asked Julius what my wedding gown looked like in the vision. He said it was white, with shimmering gold in the bodice. We both stood amazed as I shared with him that I had just purchased an ivory-white dress embroidered with gold in the bodice, and the full train was also embroidered in gold. We knew I had the wedding dress God wanted me to have and we also knew God's faithfulness and intimate involvement in the details of our life. I need to point out that the actual wedding dress was not purchased and the wedding ceremony did not occur until six years after God made the promise. God was faithful to keep his promise, but He did it according to His timetable.

One day I was sitting on my sofa, reading from Isaiah 34. I completed the chapter and shut my Bible and was about to get up when the Holy Spirit spoke to me and asked me a question: "What did you just read Debbie?" I was shocked and also ashamed by His questioning because the truth was I was clueless as to what I had read. I was just proud of the fact that I had completed my daily Bible reading. I answered the Holy Spirit, "I don't know what I read Lord, but at least I did read." He responded, "Read It Again." I immediately opened my Bible back to the Isaiah 34 and began to read intently, trying to figure out why God told me to read it again. I read each verse slowly, seeking comprehension of what I was reading, and listening for the voice of the Holy Spirit. I got to verse 16 and I knew why He had arrested my attention. It says, "Look in the scroll of the LORD and read: None of these will be missing, not one will lack her mate. For it is his mouth that has given the order, and his Spirit will gather them together." (NIV) Peace and joy began to flood my soul as I realized God was releasing me to trust him for a marriage partner and that the Holy Spirit would bring us together. God made me a personal promise from His Word of a marriage partner. When that personal word came from God, which by the way was two years after God spoke Psalm 45 to me, my faith for a husband began to develop. My assurance that God had a husband for me became my reality even though at that time I had no evidence of him in the natural realm. That personal word from God gave me assurance, it gave me peace and joy, and I waited with confident expectation and joyful anticipation for God to reveal His promise to me.

You too must receive a personal word from God that will develop your faith for a marriage partner. It is not enough to just want a husband; you must exercise faith for a husband. God may speak a specific scripture to you, as He did for me, or He may give you a peaceful assurance that He has a marriage partner for you. Your desire for marriage, as you continue to delight yourself in God, living for Him, obeying His will and instructions for your life, will cause God to order your footsteps right to that person. A hallmark of real faith is obedience. Obeying God's instructions is an indicator of your trust in His plan and wisdom for your life. James 2:26 says, "For as the human body apart from the spirit is lifeless, so faith apart from [its] works of obedience is also dead." For example, you may have a strong desire to be married, but instead of God permitting you to meet that special person, He calls you to a foreign mission field, where there are no eligible prospects for marriage. You obey God and answer the call and spend the next six months of your life in a poverty–stricken African city or village. On the plane, returning from the mission trip, you just happen to sit next to the youth pastor of a thriving church in your hometown—and he ends up being God's choice for you. If you had not exercised faith in God's ability to meet your desire, and demonstrated that trust by answering the call to the mission field, you never would have had the opportunity to meet the youth pastor on the airplane. Your faith was evidenced by your obedience and your obedience landed you God's promise, a marriage partner.

To keep your faith alive while God has you waiting, identify what you are trusting God to bring you in a marriage partner. Let the Holy Spirit mold your desires so that you don't ask for things God will not provide. James 4:3 says, "[Or] you do ask [God for them] and yet fail to receive, because you ask with wrong purpose and evil, selfish motives. Your intention is [when you get what you desire] to spend it in sensual pleasures." God is interested in providing us with answers to prayer that ultimately bring Him glory. So before you ask God for a marriage partner, you should have some idea of what kind of marriage partner would bring God glory. Keeping this is mind, your criteria should become much more related to character, integrity and kingdom productivity and much less related to outward traits that diminish with time. When I got married the first time, the only thing I asked God to give me was a saved man with a fair complexion and curly hair. I got a husband with a fair complexion and plenty of black curly hair. What I did not get were many of the qualities necessary to have a successful marriage. My faith got me just what I asked for!

To give you an example of how God changed me and molded my desires, let me share with you the type of marriage partner I trusted God for the second time.

The Husband I Asked God To Give Me

- ✟ Intimate with the Spirit of God
- ✟ Hates sin
- ✟ Loves righteousness
- ✟ Demonstrates integrity
- ✟ Demonstrates disciplined lifestyle
- ✟ Financially established
- ✟ Hunger for God's Word

✞ Passion for the place of prayer

✞ God–given, Holy Ghost-inspired revelation of what it means for Christ to love the church and give Himself – and he presents himself to me giving and having prayed about his involvement with me and believes the Lord has spoken

✞ Desires a courtship marked by outlandish holiness – no kissing until at the altar

✞ Transparent and able to communicate openly and honestly

✞ Vision for full-time ministry

✞ Romantic

✞ Has adult children who have been raised to serve the Lord and are in agreement with their Father's decision to marry me

✞ Does not snore

My list is a reflection of a number of things. First and foremost, this is what I needed God to give me in order to ensure that my marriage brings Him honor and glory. Second, this list reflects my level of understanding of what it takes to make a successful marriage. Finally, the list reflects personal things that are important for me to have. I was sexually promiscuous before God saved me and gave me a desire for His Word. I desired to make the devil pay as much as I possibly could for stealing my purity by having a courtship marked by outlandish sexual purity this time around! I did not want to have memories of sexual intimacy before our marriage, where I was left with feelings of guilt and shame. I did not want to be a rerun on my wedding night, like something that had been seen and used before, but an unopened gift for Julius with all the anticipation and excitement that comes with that. I wanted to be able to let people know that even if you have made mistakes in this area, God can restore you and give you a brand new beginning.

Notice I only had one physical characteristic on my list: I wanted a husband who did not snore. That is extremely important because I find it impossible to sleep in the same room with someone who snores loudly, and when I don't get adequate sleep I am very irritable and difficult to get along with. Neither did I did ask God for a certain type of hair, height, weight or complexion. Not that I would not have taken someone who was very handsome and athletic, but there were things more important for me to have that I knew would glorify God. Because my highest desire was to glorify God, rather than meeting my own selfish, sensual desires, God gave me just what I asked for. Julius was everything I asked for, and our courtship had the purity I desired. Our first kiss was at the altar, during our wedding ceremony. We had several very passionate embraces during our engagement but we saved that first kiss for our wedding ceremony. Because I set that as my goal and confessed it regularly for years before it happened, it guided my behavior during our courtship. There were times when our passionate embraces could have led to much more, but my confession had become my conviction and it kept me. If I had it to do all over again I would not have even permitted passionate embraces, because there is something about purity that is so awesome.

When Julius contacted me for the first time to initiate our courtship, he did just as I had trusted God for him to do. He called and informed me that God had dealt with him about pursuing a long-term relationship with me. He said he wanted to take me out to dinner and he asked me to pray and seek God's confirmation.

Daily, we seek to pattern our marriage after the relationship between Christ and the church. My husband recently began pastoring a church, and he has an awesome vision to impact the Kingdom of God in a significant way. As I shared earlier, he loves to pray and regularly wakes up at 6:00 A.M. to worship God and pray. Sometimes he kneels for over an hour, just worshipping God in song. Julius communicates openly about everything. I have married friends who have shared that their husbands refuse to talk to them, especially about things that may be causing them stress. That is not the case with Julius. He is very open and tells me freely what his thoughts are. When we need to discuss a challenging situation, he is careful to listen to my thoughts and opinion and then he also freely shares his viewpoint. Except his mortgage for a newly built home, he had no debt (neither did I). My husband has three adult children who love the Lord and serve with him in the ministry. All three of the children were pleased with their Father's decision to marry me. There is only one item on my list I did not get: On occasion my husband does snore. When I asked God why He did not give me that, I believe he said: "Continue to stand in faith." So that's what I have done. But to very honest, his snoring is mild and hardly bothers me at all. The other joy my husband has brought into my life far outweighs the mild snoring. God gave me the desires He molded in my heart. And even though I didn't ask God for good looks, my husband is quite handsome.

If you have not made your list of what you are asking God for, I encourage you to spend some time in prayer, asking the Holy Spirit what kind of marriage partner would glorify Him. Ask the Holy Spirit to mold your desires, make your list as an act of your faith in God, and then begin to praise God that He will answer. Remember to never settle for less than what you are trusting God for, because your desires have been molded from God's heart, and He will never create a desire within you that He is not willing and able to provide. When you enter into relationships that don't agree with your list, you block God from sending His real blessing to you. It also indicates you don't trust God to keep his promise to you and remember it is impossible to please God unless you trust Him.

Take your list on a regular basis and thank and praise God for your marriage partner. Praise is another act of obedience, a work of faith that demonstrates your trust in God. Praising God in advance says, "God I trust you to fulfill this promise to me." Praise creates confidence, expectation and joy, even when you see nothing in the natural to indicate you are going to meet this type of person and get married.

When exercising faith for a marriage partner, remember that God has an appointed time for every blessing, and He is never a minute early or never a minute late. Galatians 6:9 says,

> And let us not lose heart and grow weary and faint in acting nobly and doing right, for in due time and at the appointed season we shall reap, if we do not loosen and relax our courage and faint.

If you are exercising faith for a marriage partner based on a personal word from God, and you are demonstrating that faith through obedience, you need not grow weary in doing well, because God has already targeted a season for your blessing. God has predetermined your time to meet your marriage partner. Praise produces patience, marked by joy, confidence and expectation. Hebrews 10:36 says, "For you have need of steadfast patience and endurance, so that you may perform and fully accomplish the will of God, and thus receive and carry away [and enjoy to the full] what is promised." Faith—initiated through a word from God, bolstered by prayer, marked by obedience and patience, and demonstrated through praise—will produce the promise of a marriage partner from God!

One other indicator of your faith is what you speak. Hebrews 11:3 says, "By faith we understand that the worlds [during the successive ages] were framed (fashioned, put in order, and equipped for their intended purpose) by the word of God, so that what we see was not made out of things which are visible." God's word produced God's will: God spoke the world into existence. You too must speak your wife or husband into existence. Regular ongoing faith-filled confessions, based on God's Word will produce your husband or wife. As God molded my specific desires for a marriage partner, He also gave me this word-based confession I made on a regular basis.

My Husband and Marriage Confession

Father, I thank you that in the name of Jesus you have fashioned and formed for me a man of God who hates sin and loves righteousness, a man with Christ-like character and integrity. Father, I thank you that my husband has a passion for the place of prayer and a hunger for the Word of God! I thank you that he has a vision for full-time ministry. I thank you that He is obedient and submissive to authority. He has a God-given, Holy Ghost-inspired revelation of what it means for Christ to love the church and give Himself I thank you that He is financially established and has excellent communication skills.

I thank you also, Father, that you are forming me into a woman of God who submits to her husband as unto the Lord. Thank you that I am able to reverence, notice, regard, honor, prefer, venerate and esteem him; that I defer to him, praise, love and admire him exceedingly. I thank you, Father, that You give me a revelation of what it means for the church to love Christ and serve and obey You. I thank you that, at the appointed time, you will draw us together by your Spirit and we will have a courtship marked by purity, where our first kiss will be at the altar. I thank you that our wedding will glorify You and many will recognize this is Your doing and marvelous in their eyes. Our reception is a wedding feast where water will be turned into wine. Our honeymoon will be marked by anointed sex and the hallmarks of our marriage will be great sex and excellent communication. Father, I thank you that my marriage will bring honor and glory to your great name by exemplifying the relationship between Christ and the church.

Faith-filled confessions create the environment for the fulfillment for your promise and keep you encouraged during the waiting period. Failure to exercise faith leads many to make destructive comments, such as, "I will never find a husband; there are no men in my church." Or, "I will never be married; none of the women in my church are interested in me." Both of those statements may be facts, but if you are trusting God and have a Word from the Lord, God is not moved by your current circumstances; God is moved by your faith in His promise. Stay in faith and watch God's faithfulness. Romans 4: 18-20 says,

> [For Abraham, human reason for] hope being gone, hoped in faith that he should become the father of many nations, as he had been promised, So [numberless] shall your descendants be. He did not weaken in faith when he considered the [utter] impotence of his own body, which was as good as dead because he was about a hundred years old, or [when he considered] the barrenness of Sarah's [deadened] womb. No unbelief or distrust made him waver (doubtingly question) concerning the promise of God, but he grew strong and was empowered by faith as he gave praise and glory to God, Fully satisfied and assured that God was able and mighty to keep His word and to do what He had promised.

Based on what you see in your circumstances, like Abraham, you may feel you have no human reason to hope right now. But do what Abraham did; keep right on hoping for God to manifest your marriage partner, don't weaken in faith because the odds are against you; strengthen your faith by praising God. God honored Abraham's faith, God honored my faith and God will honor your faith.

My faith-filled confessions not only landed me a marriage partner who was the desire of my heart, but also an anointed wedding. Almost everyone who attended our wedding said it was the best wedding they ever attended and that it made them want to praise God for His goodness. The wedding brought glory to God. Many said only the Lord could have brought the two of us together. The theme of the wedding was from Psalm 118:23, which says, "This is from the Lord and his doing; it is marvelous in our eyes." Several young, adult single men at the wedding said seeing the wedding forever changed them. (If you would like to receive a copy of our wedding DVD, see the back of the book for details.)

Maintaining our purity until our wedding day and night has brought one of the most incredible blessings I have ever experienced. I will forever remember and cherish the first kiss my husband gave me as those who love us and support us watched and cheered at God's goodness. I will never forget the look my husband gave me the first time he saw me in my wedding lingerie and our first moments of sexual passion as husband and wife.

We have embarked on a phenomenal journey of sexual intimacy that increases in fulfillment the longer we are married.

One other point: If you believe in the gift of prophecy, and someone speaks a prophetic word to you regarding getting married or about marrying a specific purpose, I caution you against being led by the prophecy alone. Give God an opportunity to confirm His Word to you and then accept the prophecy by faith. God may be using the prophecy to encourage you during your season of waiting, but He does not expect you to make the prophecy come true. For example, if someone speaks a prophetic word to you that you will be married by next year this time, don't buy the dress and rent the hall; wait before God and make sure the person is marriage material. If someone says you are going to marry a certain person and the person is not currently marriage material, then ask God to prepare that person to be marriage material and wait until it's done before you plan your wedding.

Chapter 11

Can You See The Lover In Him/Her?

Insight into God's love is incredibly important for anyone desiring to be marriage material. There are four Greek words for love, and all four of them are operational in a strong marriage relationship, and so it is important that potential marriage partners have a working knowledge of each type and be willing to grow in their understanding and wisdom of all four as they enter a marriage relationship.

1. Storge: Affection that results from a pure motive demonstrated through a hug, a kiss, or another expression of genuine affection
2. Eros: Sexual attraction and romantic love
3. Phileo: Friendship or brotherly love
4. Agape: Unconditional love

According to the Web site divorcehope.com,

When all four types of love operate in a marriage, the marriage is complete. A picture of a complete marriage is a husband and wife who lay down their life for each other (agape love) no matter how many times the other offends them or causes them to have ill feelings. They both have tender affection toward each other (phileo love). They enjoy each other's company because they're best friends. Because they enjoy each other so much, they hug, kiss, hold hands and do nice things for their mate (storge love). Because their hearts are filled with agape, phileo and storge, a warm passionate desire arises within both of them to enjoy each other sexually (eros). Now, that kind of God-centered marriage will weather ANY storm. We must nurture and protect ALL of these different kinds of love in our marriage. Negligence of any kind of love leaves a gaping hole in our relationship.

The Holy Spirit has placed within each believer the capacity to love, utilizing each type of love. Romans 5:5b says, "[F]or God's love has been poured out in our hearts through the Holy Spirit Who has been given to us." While you are growing in your intimacy with the Lord, you will grow in your ability to express love in the various expressions of love He has provided. The Holy Spirit will instruct you through the Word of God about each aspect of love and then in the appropriate seasons of your life provide you with an opportunity to develop and demonstrate each type of love. The greater the degree of maturity you have in living the love life, the more easily you will adapt to the give-and-take involved in every successful marriage. A genuine revelation and understanding of love will compel you to make adjustments to maintain harmony in your marriage.

To determine whether you can see the lover in a potential mate or in your self, evaluate interpersonal relationships with family, coworkers and neighbors. Does the person endeavor to live out the characteristics of love outlined in 1 Corinthians 13:4-8?

- Love endures long
- Love is patient and kind
- Love is never envious
- Love never boils over with jealousy
- Love is not conceited (arrogant and inflated with pride)
- Love is not boastful
- Love does not display itself haughtily
- Love does not insist on its own rights or its own way
- Love is not self-seeking
- Love is not touchy, fretful and resentful
- Love takes no account of evil done to it or pays attention to a suffered wrong
- Love rejoices when right and truth prevail
- Love bears up under anything and everything that comes
- Love is ready to believe the best in every person
- Love hopes are fadeless under all circumstances
- Love endures everything without weakening
- Love never fails, fades or becomes obsolete

As you read through this list of qualities that exemplify love you may be thinking, "You must want me to marry Jesus, because no human being can measure up to that list." No, that's not what I am thinking, but I do believe you and the person you marry should be endeavoring to develop these qualities. Demonstrating love should not be foreign to you. Your potential spouse should not be someone who holds onto bitterness, unforgiveness and anger. Your potential spouse should not be consistently short-tempered and rude with coworkers and neighbors. If that's the behavior this person is demonstrating in other key relationships, then that may be what you have to look forward to in your marriage.

When I remarried I could not go down that list and say that I had achieved maturity in every area, but I could tell my husband these are the areas I am working on, and I need the Holy Spirit's help to mature. I was able to tell Julius how hard it used to be for me not to take account of an evil done to me and pay attention to a wrong I had suffered. I shared that when someone hurts or offends me I have to work hard at just letting it go. I was able to share with him that God had used difficult people in corporate America and in ministry to cause me to grow in my ability to demonstrate this aspect of love, but that I still require a tremendous amount of grace to live it out. I learned and continue to perfect the ability to overlook and accept the shortcomings of others without allowing them to cause me to act out of character. I now know that many of these experiences God used to prepare me to be a lover to Julius. When Julius and I work closely together on a ministry project and we are not seeing eye to eye, I am amazed at my level of patience with my husband, which really sets the stage for us to work through it, get into agreement and move forward. If the Holy Spirit had not sent me to the school of love and I did not pass a few courses before I got married, I am convinced our fights and disagreements would be much more frequent, intense and unresolved.

For those of you that are contemplating marrying a specific person right now, I encourage you to review the list carefully, evaluating whether you can see yourself exhibiting and demonstrating those qualities to that person for the rest of your life. For example, can you see yourself being patient with the person you currently want to marry for the rest of your life every time he mismanages money the way he (or she) currently does? This is what marriage means. I will exhibit and demonstrate the qualities of love toward a person no matter what that person does. I believe if people would evaluate their potential marriage partner and marriage like this, we could curtail the number of struggling marriages and divorces.

I know some of you are thinking that type of evaluation is not fair because people do change and sometimes marriage makes them change for the better. I don't choose to argue that point with you. The fact is that marriage is a lifelong covenant relationship. Wisdom would dictate that you would be better off entering the relationship with as few significant problem areas as possible.

There are two other key areas you should inspect in your own life and in the life of your potential marriage partner to see if the foundational seeds for being a lover are in place. The first is obedience. If you want to know if a person is growing in his ability to love, evaluate his obedience to God, His Word, and God's delegated authority, such as a pastor, parent or boss. Obedience is the criteria God uses to evaluate whether we love Him. John 14:23a says, "Jesus answered, If a person [really] loves Me, he will keep My word [obey My teaching]." In order to obey God's Word you must possess the ability to demonstrate the attributes I just identified. For example to demonstrate love to an unsaved coworker that lied about you to rally for a promotion that you both wanted would require you to obey God's word, which instructs us to love our enemies and pray for those who use us. In order to do that you cannot keep remembering and rehearsing an offense. You must be quick to forgive and move on.

The other fruit you can inspect is the person's giving record to determine their capacity to love. Observe whether the person gives sacrificially, particularly to needs related to God's Kingdom. Will they sacrifice their finances, time, resources and gifts to ensure the needs of the Kingdom are met, or will they selfishly withhold what they could freely give and let the Kingdom of God suffer? A person's giving record is a real indicator of their understanding of love. God chose to demonstrate the love He has for us by giving. John 3:16 says, "For God so greatly loved and dearly prized the world that He [even] gave up His only begotten (unique) Son that whoever believes in (trusts in, clings to, relies on) Him shall not perish (come to destruction, be lost) but have eternal (everlasting) life." When a person has grown in their ability to demonstrate love through giving, particularly sacrificially (not just giving with a view of what's in it for me, but giving with a view of what is in it for another person), they are ready to be marriage material. They will give whatever they need to make their marriage successful – time, money, obedience, faithfulness, silence, gifts, forgiveness – whatever!

Chapter 12

What Are You Looking At And Where Did It Come From?

S adly, marriage has lost its appeal to many, and largely because we don't see very many examples of successful marriages. If you have never seen a living example of what God intended marriage to be, it will be difficult for you to implement it. Many adults enter marriage never having seen a successful marriage or family in operation. They want to be married, and they know they want something better than what their parents had, but they really aren't sure what it's supposed to look like. So, even though we enter a marriage determined to produce something better than what we saw and experienced, our best efforts may be futile because all we know to do is what we have seen, which in most cases is a bad example that may have ended in divorce. When trying to decide on a person to marry, we may select the bad example we observed and not the desire we dreamed about. What will ultimately guide us is what our minds have seen and developed as longstanding images. When faced with the same marital pressures our parents dealt with, the responses that will surface are not what we want, but what we know, what we have seen. I knew I did not want to marry a man like my mother did, and I did not want to have a marriage relationship like she had, marked by ongoing mental, physical and verbal abuse as well as adultery and alcoholism. I remember openly declaring I will never have a marriage like my mother's. I wanted something better than what she had and yet, in many ways, my first marriage resembled the kind of marriage my mother had. This is why it is vitally important that we see examples of long-term, Godly courtship and marriage. We need to see it done the right way long enough that it transforms our images, our thinking and ultimately our actions. Before you decide that you are marriage material you should make sure you know what a good marriage looks like.

In order to qualify as marriage material, you should allow the Holy Spirit to lead you to a setting where you have an opportunity over a period of time to observe Godly examples of marriages and families. One of the best instruction methods is observation. The local church God has sent you to may be the place where you spend your season of observation. Many single adults miss this season because, instead of observing happily married couples, they become jealous and feel left out. God may have intentionally placed you in a setting where there are lots of couples and families so you can observe them.

There was tremendous and compelling teaching about marriage and family at the church I attended when I began to take my relationship with Jesus seriously, and consequently I had several examples of Godly marriages constantly before me. The one that meant the most to me was the one I carefully observed between my former pastor and his wife. He taught the principles of a Godly marriage from the pulpit and then he endeavored to live them out in his personal life. His children's lives convinced me that he was living what he taught. The level of stability and success his children had while they were single, the mates they selected as marriage partners and the marriages they currently have reveal the quality of marriage my pastor and his wife have. Matthew 11:19 b says, "Yet wisdom is justified and vindicated by what she does (her deeds) and by her children."

I didn't just see the public side of their marriage. One time I also traveled on a two-week missions trip with my pastor and his wife to Ethiopia. I had an opportunity to see their marriage close up. I saw them argue, and I saw them resolve their differences. I saw her submit to him even when she didn't want to. I saw him overlook her faults (mine, too). I saw her respect him and make sure he was prepared for ministry. I saw him give her opportunity to use her gifts. These observations transformed how I viewed marriage. I began to realize that marriage is not about one person coming into my life to make me happy, but two imperfect people coming together working very hard at accepting one another's differences, shortcomings and at the same time endeavoring to help the other person accomplish God's will for their life.

Over the years, I have seem him provide leadership to his wife and family. It seems to me over time my Pastor and his wife grew more in love with each other and their marriage got stronger. They have been married for about forty years, and my former Pastor proudly admits that she is the only woman he has been intimate with during their entire marriage. This was especially important for me to see because while I was growing up I seldom saw strong male leadership exhibited in my home. The women in our family were the strong leaders. When God wants you to be married and you allow the Holy Spirit to lead you, God will permit you to see what you need to see, so you become what you need to be.

"Bad Marriages Are Just A Part Of My Family!"

Another reason you may not qualify as marriage material is the impact generational curses have on your ability to select a good marriage partner and to have a successful marriage. If your life has a generational curse that has not been broken by the power of God through the blood and name of Jesus, you are not marriage material. Multiple divorces within a family line may indicate a generational curse. Generational curses are judgments that are passed on to individuals because of sins perpetuated in a family in a number of generations. Exodus 20:5 -6 says,

> You shall not bow down to them or worship them; for I, the Lord your God, am a jealous God, punishing the children for the sin of the fathers to the third and fourth generation of those who hate me, but showing love to a thousand generations of those who love me and keep my commandments. (NIV)

For example your great grandfather, grandfather and father all divorced their wives during middle age; or your great grandmother, all her sisters, your grandmother and your mother and all her sisters married alcoholics who physically abused them. These scenarios may be examples of generational curses. Before seriously considering marriage, make sure you have assessed whether you are operating under a generational curse and, if so, break it. Generational curses are broken by repentance and deliverance. If you believe you are bound by a generational curse, here is an example of a prayer you should pray:

Lord Jesus Christ, I confess to you all of the sins of my ancestors on all sides of all of my families, repenting of all of their sins, and in particular, of all of their sins that brought the curse of ungodly mate selection, problem-ridden marriages and divorce into our family line. I repent of all of those ancestral sins and ask for Your forgiveness for what they did. I ask for forgiveness for whomever they may have hurt as a consequence of these sins. I now break this genera-

tional curse off myself and my offspring, breaking all ties and past sins. I decree that we are free and this curse is broken, for it is written that in that day you shall decree a thing and it shall come to pass.

Your Word says that where there is Christ, there is liberty. Your Word says that He whom the Son sets free is indeed free. I stand on Your Word, Lord Jesus Christ, decreeing this generational curse is broken once and for all, and I release the blessing upon myself to find God's choice for a marriage partner and to experience the marriage that honors and glorifies you, Father, and demonstrates the relationship that Christ is to have to the church. I apply the precious and pure blood of Jesus to my marriage partner and future marriage and remind the angel of death and destruction you are not to cross the blood. Now I do thank and praise you in advance for my marriage and marriage partner that glorifies you, Father!

Chapter 13

Would You Marry You?

Well, would you? Marry someone just like you, that is? Most of the time when considering marriage we focus on what we want in the other person more than what we bring to the partnership. We want the potential mate to look a certain way, act a certain way and enjoy the activities we enjoy. Have you ever turned the table, and looked at yourself and asked, "What do I have to offer a potential marriage partner?" That's much harder to do because to answer that question truthfully we have to examine ourselves honestly. I am amazed at how many single adults want more in a marriage partner than they can offer. Women sometimes want a very athletic man, but they don't exercise and take care of their own body. Men want a good housekeeper, but they don't cleanup after themselves. Women want men who have achieved financial success, yet their financial portfolio is marked by debt. When the expectations you place on your potential marriage partner are greater than the expectations you place on yourself, you are not setting a foundation for a successful marriage. Anything you expect from a marriage partner you should be prepared to provide. If you want a person to weigh a certain amount, is it because you endeavor to keep your weight within a certain range? If you want someone who is well groomed, is it because that's how you are? If you want someone who keeps their home and car clean and organized, is it because you work hard at keeping your home and car clean? When you want more than you are willing to give, conflict will arise. It's not fair to expect someone to do something you are not willing to do for yourself.

When considering expectations you have for a potential marriage partner, be the best you can be and then you have a right to expect the best. Don't expect more than you are prepared to offer.

Also, don't make the common mistake of believing that once you have married a person, you will be able to change that person. The old saying *"What you see is what you get"* certainly applies to marriage. A person's weaknesses and faults before marriage will not automatically change because they get married to you. God did not design marriage to change people. That's His job. We see in 2 Corinthians 5:17, "Therefore if any person is [ingrafted] in Christ (the Messiah) he is a new creation (a new creature altogether); the old [previous moral and spiritual condition] has passed away. Behold the fresh and new has come!" There can be no transformation of a person apart from an intimate relationship with Jesus. You can only qualify as marriage material when your expectations about your potential marriage partner are fair. You must bring to the union as much as you expect. Don't expect to mold your spouse after marriage.

Chapter 14

Dating Your Way To The Altar

M any singles use their success at dating a person as the primary indicator to qualify them as marriage material. You hear them make statements such as, "We have gone out for over a year and we really have a good time together"; "I just love being with her"; "He makes me feel like a different person." I recommend before you allow a track record of successful dating to lead you to the altar a more in-depth analysis of your dating needs to occur. Dating many times creates artificial relationship circumstances. It may be difficult to determine how a person acts under pressure, or judge their character over a candle-lit dinner—unless the candle starts a fire! If he runs from the room, screaming, "Every man for himself," he's probably not a good marriage choice.

Most often, during dating we put our best foot forward; we're on our best behavior. Rarely during a date would a person tell you, "I am slob and I hate picking up after myself," or "I am a compulsive spender and stay in debt; creditors are hounding me." This is the type of information you need to know before getting married, but dating may not allow it to come to the surface. If this type of information comes up at all during dating it usually happens after the emotional attachments have developed as a result of the close contact during dating. Then you may find yourself wanting to ignore this type of information or deceive yourself into believing it will change once you are married. Dating alone doesn't always give you the information you need to determine whether a person is ready to handle the responsibility of marriage. In fact, dating may masquerade a person's true character, particularly if strong emotional attachments and sexual intimacy are a part of the dating relationship. No one wants to deal with potentially negative attributes that could hinder or stop the relationship when the relationship is bringing you so much pleasure.

I know the next question you can hardly wait to ask is, "How can I get to know people, if I don't date?" My response to you may sound "religious," nevertheless it will ensure that you find "Mr. or Miss Right" and also make sure you qualify as marriage material when they show up. Proverbs 3:5-6 says, "Lean on, trust in, and be confident in the Lord with all your heart and mind and do not rely on your own insight or understanding. In all your ways know, recognize and acknowledge Him, and He will direct and make straight and plain your paths." The Living Bible states it this way: "If you want favor with both God and man, and a reputation for good judgment and common sense, then trust the Lord completely; don't ever trust yourself. In everything you do, put God first, and he will direct you and crown your efforts with success." If you make the decision to first of all trust God's love and plan for your life enough that you will acknowledge him in all your decisions about dating, God will prepare you for marriage and make sure you get His choice. To acknowledge God means to seek God's input, to want to know what God has to say about all your dating decisions. He promises you that if you will do that, He will direct your path. God will steer you clear of dating relationships that serve no useful purpose in your life and lead you to date only people He has chosen for you. God will prevent you from becoming like an article of clothing on a sales rack, selected, tried on for size and returned if it doesn't fit well. If you only date people God leads you to date, you can avoid the mistakes and disappointment that dating so often brings. You want God's direction because, according to Jeremiah 29:11, God knows the plans He has for your life. "For I know the thoughts and plans that I have for you says the Lord, thoughts and plans for welfare and peace and not for evil, to give you hope in your final outcome."

The next comment you may have is, "But I have asked God about dating specific people and He doesn't say anything, so I just assume it must be okay." My response to your comment is, "God knows how to say 'yes,' and God knows how to say 'no.'" If He doesn't say either, don't assume God means yes. Remember back to when you were a child. You knew that a parent's silence to your request didn't necessarily mean their answer was yes. Silence usually means you should wait until your parents are ready to talk. You knew you would be in trouble if you acted without your parent's approval. It is the same way with God. When God is quiet to a question you ask Him (you didn't get an inward witness or the manifestation of a natural circumstance that would reveal to you His will) then wait for God to reveal Himself. God is not rude and will not harshly ignore you, but will wisely guide you if you let Him. Over time, God shall reveal His will so that it becomes clear, or He will cause natural circumstances to happen in such away that you will have the information you need to make the right decision. You still need the grace to obey what God tells you, but God will never leave you in the dark about His will. God is more committed to you having a successful marriage than you are.

Also remember you always have God's Word to guide you. For example, if an unbeliever asks you out on date, you have God's specific guidance in 2 Corinthians 6:14-15:

Do not be unequally yoked with unbelievers [do not make mismated alliances with them or come under a different yoke with them, inconsistent with your faith]. For what partnership have right living and right standing with God with iniquity and lawlessness? Or how can light have fellowship with darkness? What harmony can there be between Christ and Belial [the devil]? Or what has a believer in common with an unbeliever?

According to God's Word, when a saved person and an unsaved person come together in a dating relationship they don't have anything in common. This is not to say that you can't witness to an unsaved person, but witnessing should not include going out for dinner and allowing yourself to become emotionally attached to that person. Many times this is very difficult to prevent. Remember my initial contacts with my first husband were as a believer and an unbeliever. I led him to the Lord. Had I stopped the relationship at that point I would have been fine. But I permitted myself to become emotionally and physically attracted to him and the results were devastating.

I can remember several times in my single life after my divorce when men seemed interested in me or I had an interest in them, but I was not sure if it was God's will. I asked God, and when He responded with silence, I chose not to pursue the relationship. In some cases I was being obedient, but in other cases I was afraid to take the risk. Either way, it was easier for me to do nothing. But as I waited and chose not to act, over time, God showed me something in that person's character or the person began to openly see another woman and then I knew what God's will was for me.

When God revealed who my husband would be, He left no room for doubt. He made His will perfectly clear to me, but He did it on His timetable. Earlier I shared that after my divorce, when I began to ask God if it was His will for me to remarry, He made it perfectly clear that was not His will for me at that time. I was fasting and praying and seeking to hear His voice and He answered right away, leading me by His Word. He answered me quickly because I needed to know quickly so that I could begin to conform my life to His direction. If He had not made it perfectly clear that He wanted me to pursue my relationship with Him—rather than pursuing marriage—I would not have been focused. People who aren't focused in the direction God is leading miss what God has for them. If I had not lined my life up with God's agenda at that time I would have missed God. I would have missed the opportunity to establish the ministry of Singles Pleasing The Lord. I would have missed the opportunity to be a radio and television host and a successfully married woman!

When God first told me He did not want me to marry, He was teaching me obedience. Then, four years later, He updated his plan and told me I was going to marry again but didn't tell me who or when. He was teaching me faith and trust.

Two years after God told me I was going to get married again, He revealed to me who it was. This was two years before He revealed it to my husband and my husband pursued me. God chose a Friday Night Prayer Meeting at my local church to share with me who He had selected as my husband. Julius, newly widowed at the time, was sitting several rows in front of me. I had no attraction to him whatsoever. In fact, I had worked along side him in the ministry for years and did not really like him. I was saddened by the sudden death of his wife, a dear friend of mine, but did not consider him an eligible marriage partner. I knew him to be a solid man of God, who genuinely loved the Lord, but definitely not my type. While sitting at that prayer meeting, as I was casually observing my husband sitting in front of me, God said, "That is your husband." I immediately dismissed that as a fleeting thought that had no merit. I did not see this man as someone I wanted to marry. In fact that thought did not agree with me at all. In spite of my trying to dismiss that thought, it continued to come to my mind. During my drive home, and even as I prepared for bed, I kept hearing it over and over, "That is your husband." I would dismiss the thought and it would come back.

I went to bed, and when I awoke the next morning the first thought that greeted me was, "That is your husband." Then the Holy Spirit asked me to review what I had asked God to give me in a husband. Two years before I had made a list identifying the type of husband I wanted God to give me. I saved this list on my computer. I pulled up this list (which I shared in an earlier chapter) on my computer and began to review it. As I did, I was amazed at the fact that this man personified everything on my list I asked for, even though I did not like him. I knew God was trying to get my attention. Realizing it was God, but not sure if I wanted to accept it, I told God, "If this is you talking to me, then you must orchestrate it, I am not going to do anything." Two years later, God spoke to Julius, and our courtship began. Successful dating alone did not convince me that my husband and I were marriage material. As I acknowledged God, He ordered my footsteps to my husband.

Julius and I dated for eight months before we married, but only after we knew it was God who had brought us together. Our first date he was the perfect gentlemen, opening car doors, bringing me flowers, taking me to an upscale seafood restaurant and, most special of all, praying as we started and closed the date. During the date we talked openly, but we still were not totally transparent. He was trying to put his best foot forward, and so was I. There was no way I could have confirmed that He was God's choice for me based on that type of dating.

We used our dates as time to prepare for our new life together. Frequently over a meal we spent time discussing how we were going to bring two ministries and two families together, what our current financial portfolios looked like, what are financial goals were, how we were going to move me a single woman who had lived alone for thirteen years in a two-bedroom apartment into a newly built home with four bedrooms, our expectations regarding sexual intimacy, his family and friends, my family and friends and their responses to our marriage, our long-term and short-term goals and our strengths and weaknesses. Some of our dating included time with close friends and family members, although we did not make our relationship public until we had a final blessing from my pastor. Our dating was marked by fun and enjoyment, but we also used the time wisely, preparing for our married life. We also planned a wedding with a guest list of over 200. I share that because so often engaged couples spend more time planning the wedding than they do the marriage. The wedding is one day, the marriage is a lifetime commitment and consequently the planning and preparation a couple does should reflect that.

So often I believe God meets us according to our expectations. Many of you may struggle with the idea of dating only after your marriage partner has been revealed to you by God. You would prefer to discover and have God confirm that person to you through dating experiences. God is surely creative and powerful enough to do both, but it really boils down to your expectations and your readiness. My expectations of God changed after I heard several testimonies of God revealing and confirming marriage partners to people before they dated. They shared that before their marriage partners took them out on a date they knew God had chosen them to be their mate. They were not dating hoping that this person was going to ultimately want to marry them. When I heard those testimonies I realized the possibilities that exist when you trust God, and they inspired me to change my expectations about how God would reveal my potential marriage partner to me. I did not just want to date people with the hopes that it might turn into marriage. I wanted to know God had spoken to me and the person I was dating about our long-term future, before we dated. I began to trust God for that. My expectations created my reality. Matthew 9:29 says, "According to your faith and trust and reliance [on the power invested in Me] be it done to you." Besides that I had had such negative experiences with dating. I easily developed emotional attachments with men that never ended in a marriage proposal and an engagement ring, but rather in disappointment, rejection guilt and pain. In fact I had a track record of pain from dating, so I wanted to stay clear of dating. I just wanted God to bring my husband when He was ready. That's what I believed God for and that's exactly what happened.

Besides that the Bible seems to support that God will show you who your mate is, confirm it and bring the two of you together. That's what God did for Isaac and Rebekkah. The beautiful love story is unfolded in Genesis 24. When Isaac turned 40, his father Abraham released him to find a wife and get married. As custom would have it, locating this woman was the responsibility of the servant Eliezer. He had clear directions that he was not to bring Isaac a Canaanite woman, but that Isaac was to be equally yoked with a woman from his country. Eliezer recognizing how important it was for him to locate for Isaac the right bride, asked God for confirmation of his choice for Isaac. There were many women Eliezer could have chosen from that day to be Isaac's bride, but God made it obvious who his choice was. Genesis 24:13-14 says,

See, I stand here by the well of water, and the daughters of the men of the city are coming to draw water.

And let it so be that the girl to whom I say, I pray you, let down your jar that I may drink, and she replies, Drink, and I will give your camels drink also—let her be the one whom You have selected and appointed and indicated for Your servant Isaac [to be a wife to him]; and by it I shall know that You have shown kindness and faithfulness to my master.

Then we see God's response to that request in verses 17-20:

And the servant ran to meet her, and said, I pray you, let me drink a little water from your water jar. And she said, Drink, my lord; and she quickly let down her jar onto her hand and gave him a drink. When she had given him a drink, she said, I will draw water for your camels also, until they finish drinking. So she quickly emptied her jar into the trough and ran again to the well and drew water for all his camels.

God faithfully responded and led Eliezer right to Rebekah. Meanwhile, Rebekah responded favorably to the proposal, received her family's blessing and went to meet her husband. The first time Isaac laid eyes on Rebekah, he knew she was God's choice for him. There was no trial and error or rejection and pain. Success at dating is not what brought this couple together, but rather prayer, obedience, accurate leading of the Holy Spirit, and the blessing of the families of both the bride and the groom.

Chapter 15

Does Your Leader Say
You Are Ready?

Every person contemplating marriage should have in their life an authority figure who can confirm and validate they are ready for marriage. This authority figure should have wisdom and insight into what it takes to have a successful marriage. Ideally, this person should be both your parents or both your pastors. It may also be a mentor or spiritual mother or father. This need for authority applies whether you are 23 and getting married for the first time or 58 and getting married for the third time. You need a leadership figure in your life to confirm your readiness for marriage. Proverbs 11:14 states, "Where no wise guidance is, the people fall, but in the multitude of counselors there is safety." The authority figure should be a mature believer with a solid working knowledge of the God's Word, an intimate relationship with the Holy Spirit, and a strong prayer life. This person should be able to make a natural and supernatural assessment of your potential spouse's character. Ideally, this authority should be a person who has watched over your spiritual development and knows your strengths and weaknesses and is able to make an accurate assessment of your readiness for marriage.

Many people believe that being a certain age qualifies them to make a decision about marriage. Being an adult is not the sole prerequisite for a successful marriage. Many adults have married based solely on the fact that they were grown and free to make choices, and today, these same grown people are living in hell or divorced!

Consulting an authority figure is important because when we are deciding on a marriage partner we lose objectivity, and strong emotional attachments cloud our ability to make wise, Spirit-led decisions. Emotions that have been stimulated by an attractive member of the opposite sex speak loudly. They cause us to overlook red flags, signals and warning signs that this person may not be right for us. We convince ourselves that the red flags are not important, or we believe we will be able to change the person or situation once we are married. During this time deception is very possible. We can't hear the voice of the Holy Spirit because we feel such passion. We are dreaming about the romance and the wedding, and anticipating the honeymoon. We don't want to hear anything that will keep us from our emotional and physical desires. Emotions become blinded by pleasure. Emotion management is extremely challenging when you've developed affection for someone. Even the most self-controlled individuals struggle to keep a level head when they are emotionally attached to someone.

When your mentor/advisor asks you questions about your potential marriage relationship, you must be completely honest. Don't withhold or give inaccurate information. Your advisor will base their advice and counsel on the information you provide, and if you are not completely truthful, your advisor can't give you the best advice. You can only gain by being honest. Whatever you're afraid to tell may be the very information they need to know to correctly counsel you. If you don't agree with their decision and advice, then spend sometime in God's presence, letting Him confirm their counsel to you. God will readily do this so that you can have peace to accept and obey them. God wants you to walk in His wisdom; He will never fault you for seeking His wisdom. James 1:5 says, "If any of you lacks wisdom, he should ask God, who gives generously to all without finding fault, and it will be given to him." (NIV) God has given you spiritual leadership to protect you. Hebrews 13:17 says,

> Obey your spiritual leaders and submit to them [continually recognizing their authority over you], for they are constantly keeping watch over your souls and guarding your spiritual welfare, as men who will have to render an account [of their trust]. [Do your part to] let them do this with gladness and not with sighing and groaning, for that would not be profitable to you [either].

Ultimately, the decision to marry or not marry rests with you and your potential marriage partner, but having the blessing of wise, Godly counsel can provide an important confirmation. The Lord does not want to withhold the right marriage partner from you. Psalms 84:11 says, "For the Lord God is a Sun and Shield; the Lord bestows [present] grace and favor and [future] glory (honor, splendor, and heavenly bliss)! No good thing will He withhold from those who walk uprightly."

Before remarrying—before even dating my new husband—I went to my former Pastor and sought his approval. I valued his opinion, I trusted his judgment, and I wanted his blessing. I believe seeking his approval this soon was not premature. I had no time or emotional energy to waste on dating the wrong person; therefore my pastor's blessing was essential to me. I knew I was a woman of destiny and God had his hand on my life for His purposes and His glory. Therefore, I could not allow myself to make unwise decisions.

When my husband asked me out for the first time, he gave me the opportunity to pray before I gave him my response. I took that opportunity even though God had already spoken to me about Julius. After I sensed God releasing me to go, I then called my pastor and asked for his counsel. My pastor gave me permission to go on only one date, and then he requested that, after the date, I bring Julius into his office for a meeting. I agreed. We did go on our first date, and, as I shared in the last chapter, it was awesome. At the end of the date I shared with Julius that we would not be able to date again until after we had a meeting with my pastor. Julius agreed to this meeting, even though at this point he had not asked me to marry him. At the meeting with my pastor, Julius shared that God had shown him through three separate vivid dreams that I would be his wife. I shared what God had shown me about him. At this point I told Julius and my pastor that I needed more time, so my pastor released us to continue to date. After a month or so of dating we went back to my pastor and shared with him that we were ready to prepare for marriage. He took us through several intense pre-marital counseling sessions. Five months later, we were married. I believe that this process is one of the major reasons I am a successfully married woman today.

Premarital counseling is very important. Make sure in these sessions financial management, effective communi-cation, in-law relationships, views on parenting and sexual intimacy are covered, because these are the areas most vulnerable to satanic influence and attack. This counseling should give you insight and wisdom on how to be successful at marriage. Living successfully within marriage is not intui-tive; you must be taught and learn by experience. Before you were permitted to drive legally, someone had to teach you and test you for a license. Before a surgeon is permitted to perform surgery he must be educated, trained and tested for a license. Before you get married you should have adequate preparation.

Learning to communicate is one of the most important skills you need to nurture before getting married. Most people aren't taught good communication skills or good conflict resolution skills. Listening skills, learning to pay attention and learning to paraphrase what has been communicated for clarification are essential skills you'll need to develop for a successful marriage. If you tend to "bottle in" your feelings, you will need to learn to talk about them, instead of stewing about them. Married couples must be able to negotiate so both can win. You won't always get your way. The more adept you become at these communication skills while single the more successful your marriage will be.

Chapter 16

Do I Have To Be Perfect?

B y now you may be asking, "Do I have to be perfect to get married?" The answer is, "No you don't have to be perfect, but you do need to be ready." What do I mean by ready? When someone is ready, they are prepared. You must be ready to make a lifelong commitment to grow. Two perfect people don't get married and have a perfect marriage. Two ready people get married and grow together, developing a marriage that glorifies God and represents the relationship that Christ and the church share.

Going into your marriage, you need to be aware of potential problem areas and be ready to "satan–proof" your marriage by adding extra protection to these areas. For example, you may have a tendency to spend inappropriately and, even though you have worked hard at getting out of debt in preparation for marriage, you know that a good sale is hard to turn down. Knowing this about yourself going into the marriage, you and your marriage partner can do what the scripture instructs us to do to avoid temptation. Matthew 26:41 says, "All of you must keep awake (give strict attention, be cautious and active) and watch and pray, that you may not come into temptation. The spirit indeed is willing, but the flesh is weak." Watch yourself carefully in this area. Don't spend behind your spouse's back; notify your spouse when you are going to shop. Watch the budget.

Readiness indicators that every person contemplating marriage should be familiar with include:

- You should be in a personal intimate relationship with the Lord.
- Your greatest desire should be to serve and please the Lord, before you consider marriage. Your life should demonstrate this through involvement in a local church or the ministry God has called you to, and utilizing your gifts and resources to advance God's Kingdom.
- You should know how to hear God's voice and be led by His Spirit.
- You should be living sexually pure.
- You should be financially established. (At a minimum you should be out of debt, and able to manage your own personal finances.)
- You should have a clear indication of the direction God is leading you in terms of your calling and career.
- You should be submitted to spiritual leadership and, if appropriate, parental leadership who are able to advise you regarding your marriage choices.
- You should have the ability to recognize a good man or woman when you see him or her. You should evaluate people's character and integrity, rather than their physical appearance. Having said that, obesity and shabbiness are physical attributes that may reflect character deficits. Am I saying obese people aren't marriage material? No. I am saying that, if you are obese you may have a discipline problem, and health issues that could make being married to you

challenging. A negative past should not necessarily disqualify a person as a potential mate. If Julius had evaluated me on my past mistakes he would not have married me. I was a sexually promiscuous young adult who had an abortion and one failed marriage Thank God, Julius did not only look at my past; he looked at how I had allowed my past to become the catalyst to change my future. He saw I embraced God and His Word passionately and permitted the Holy Spirit to transform me.

This list reveals that marriage-readiness must be evaluated and accomplished on several different levels. To be married, you must be ready spiritually, financially, emotionally, relationally, and physically. Ready people don't have perfect marriages, but they do have successful marriages.

"But I Know People Who Are Married and They Were Not Marriage Material"

Reviewing that list is probably causing you to do two things. First, you are assessing your current level of readiness. Second, you are thinking about people you know whose marriage seems good even though they did not demonstrate the level of readiness identified in this book when they got married. My response is, "I do too." However, my purpose is to establish God best; His ideal prerequisites for a strong marriage. God always establishes His ideal in His Word and then we decide how much of His ideal we will experience by our response to His Word.

Many couples enter marriage with a limited understanding of these readiness criteria, and as they grow in their understanding, and both partners are willing to adapt, adjust and change, they can still experience a successful marriage. God always meets us where we are and takes us where He wants us to go, if we let Him. God's best, however, is to have a good understanding of what it takes to have a successful marriage and bring that foundation to the altar when you say, "I do." This preparation will minimize the turmoil and difficulty that many marriages experience, particularly in the early years of marriage. It will also prepare you to handle the challenges that even the best marriages will face. Actually the longer you stay single if you are living the single life successfully the more prepared you should be to handle marriage, because you've had more time for God to prepare you. Before getting married the second time, I came to the conclusion that I had experienced too much pain and suffered too many negative consequences from having one unsuccessful marriage. I was willing to pay any price for God to make me into marriage material. It meant I had to wait longer, but the marital happiness I have now was worth the wait.

Chapter 17

Other Factors to Consider

In this society where divorce and single parenting is commonplace when considering readiness for marriage there our other factors to consider. We want to examine those factors now.

What About Your Kids?

If you desire to be married and you have children, you should not make the decision based only on your desire and readiness; you must take into consideration your children's needs and readiness. If you are ready for marriage and your children are not ready for you to be married, you are not marriage material. Attempting to force children to accept your choice for a marriage partner may only create problems for your child and your marriage.

Your child's desire for you to marry is based on their understanding of how your marriage will affect them personally. By nature, children are selfish and view life from a selfish perspective. (Some adults have that same childish perspective.) If your children believe your marriage will benefit them, they may buy into your decision to marry. If they believe marriage will detract from them in anyway, they will not readily agree to your desire to marry. Sometimes the idea of having their only parent share time with someone else makes children feel insecure and threatened, or rejected. If the child has a good relationship with your ex-partner, the child may have a greater degree of resistance to your marriage desires. The only person the child may want to see you with is that ex-partner, even if the relationship was troubled.

Forcing your child to accept your desire to marry could have disastrous long-term consequences. Children who are *forced* to accept a stepparent tend to be more needy and insecure; many struggle in school, scholastically and behaviorally. This problem is compounded and complicated when the new parent does not exercise wisdom in dealing with the child. If the new parent inappropriately disciplines the child or fails to treat the child's other parent appropriately, then the child will resent the new parent and may rebel. This rebellion could then result in a household marked by strife and confusion for the whole family.

The scripture is very clear about one thing: If you are a single parent, whether because of divorce, widowhood or any other reason, your number-one responsibility is to successfully care for your child, not to seek a marriage partner. When you do this, God will bring into your life every resource you need in order to accomplish it, including a marriage partner—if one is appropriate and needed. God will help you make that assessment. Genesis 21: 14-20 says,

> So Abraham rose early in the morning, and took bread and a skin of water; and putting it on her shoulder, he gave it and the boy to Hagar, and sent her away. Then she departed and wandered in the Wilderness of Beersheba. And the water in the skin was used up, and she placed the boy under one of the shrubs. Then she went and sat down across from him at a distance

of about a bowshot; for she said to herself, "Let me not see the death of the boy." So she sat opposite him, and lifted her voice and wept. **And God heard the voice of the lad.** Then the angel of God called to Hagar out of heaven, and said to her, "What ails you, Hagar? Fear not, for **God has heard the voice of the lad** where he is. Arise, lift up the lad and hold him with your hand, for I will make him a great nation." Then God opened her eyes, and she saw a well of water. And she went and filled the skin with water, and gave the lad a drink. So God was with the lad; and he grew and dwelt in the wilderness, and became an archer. (Emphasis added, NKJV)

Hagar's focus as a single parent was on the welfare of her child, and *as she cried* out to God on the boy's behalf, *God heard the voice of the child. God did not hear Hagar*, God heard the child. This is a significant point for every single parent. God responds to your cry and his response is first and foremost directed to your child. Single parents who have a desire to be married: Remember that God will deal with you in the best interests of your children.

So, no matter how strong your desire for marriage is, if marriage is not what is best for your child, God is not going to lead you to be married. If, however, God knows that marriage will enhance your ability to raise your child successfully, He stands ready to arrange a marriage for you. This child-focus should be the foundation for every single parent considering marriage. Has God indicated to me that in order for me to successfully raise my child I need to be married? If God has made that known to you, then trust Him to orchestrate it. God will prepare your child—and your marriage partner. If, on the other hand, you selfishly seek out a marriage partner because you are lonely, or because your sexual drive is out of control, or you are struggling financially, then your motive for marriage is wrong and you are not marriage material. You will have put your own needs over the needs of your child, and God will not be pleased.

God gives special grace to marriage partners to raise and love children who are not their own. Marrying someone who has not been given that grace makes marriage and child-rearing difficult, if not impossible.

But I've been Married Before!

When dealing with an assessment of marriage readiness the next thing that must be considered is whether you have been married before. God's original and best plan is that one man would be married to one woman until death. The current state of marriage—in the world and in the church—is a far cry from God's original plan. Divorce is commonplace, and many of these same divorcees, even though they could not stay in their first marriage, want to remarry. Listen to these very alarming statistics:

- 41% of 1st marriages end in divorce
- 60% of 2nd marriages end in divorce
- 73% of 3rd marriages end in divorce
  (Taken from Marriage and Divorce Today-1988, page 1)

According to divorcemagazine.com's statistics from the U. S. Census Bureau, the National Center for Health Statistics and Americans for Divorce reform reported that in 1997 60 percent of all remarriages ended in divorce.

The Bible has given very specific guidelines regarding remarriage, and if you don't meet these guidelines you are not marriage material. Scripture cites two cases for remarriage. The first is in Matthew 19:1-9:

Now when Jesus had finished saying these things, He left Galilee and went into the part of Judea that is beyond the Jordan; And great throngs accompanied Him, and He cured them there. And Pharisees came to Him and put Him to the test by asking, Is it lawful and right to dismiss and repudiate and divorce one's wife for any and every cause? He replied, Have you never read that He Who made them from the beginning made them male and female, And said, For this reason a man shall leave his father and mother and shall be united firmly (joined inseparably) to his wife, and the two shall become one flesh? So they are no longer two, but one flesh. What therefore God has joined together, let not man put asunder (separate). They said to Him, Why then did Moses command [us] to give a certificate of divorce and thus to dismiss and repudiate a wife? He said to them, Because of the hardness (stubbornness and perversity) of your hearts Moses permitted you to dismiss and repudiate and divorce your wives; but from the beginning it has not been so [ordained]. I say to you: whoever dismisses (repudiates, divorces) his wife, except for unchastity, and marries another commits adultery, and he who marries a divorced woman commits adultery.

Here Jesus seems to imply the only time remarriage is permissible after a divorce is when one of the marriage partners has been involved in sexual immorality. He further states that if you remarry after divorcing your spouse and the reason for the divorce was not sexual immorality, then you are committing adultery. Jesus does not mention a divorce for irreconcilable differences as a reason for divorce and subsequent remarriage. Remember, we discussed the main purpose for marriage is to demonstrate the relationship between Christ and the church. Would Christ divorce the

143

church for irreconcilable differences? No, Christ would be longsuffering and patient and trust God to intervene with His omnipotence and omniscience.

In the other scripture about remarriage, Paul writes the following:

> Now to the married I command, yet not I but the Lord: A wife is not to depart from her husband. But even if she does depart, let her remain unmarried or be reconciled to her husband. And a husband is not to divorce his wife. But to the rest I, not the Lord, say: If any brother has a wife who does not believe, and she is willing to live with him, let him not divorce her. And a woman who has a husband who does not believe, if he is willing to live with her, let her not divorce him. For the unbelieving husband is sanctified by the wife, and the unbelieving wife is sanctified by the husband; otherwise your children would be unclean, but now they are holy. But if the unbeliever departs, let him depart; a brother or a sister is not under bondage in such cases. But God has called us to peace (1 Corinthians 7:10-15 NKJV).

Paul tells us we are to remain married, even if we are married to an unbeliever, if that unbeliever chooses to stay with us. But if the unbelieving spouse departs, Paul seems to imply you are free to divorce because God does not want you in bondage to that relationship but rather to have peace. In my opinion this would also imply if your unbelieving spouse abandons you; then you are free to divorce and remarry. Some may say I am reading into the scripture by coming to that conclusion. I choose to believe I am looking into the character of God and believe that to remain unmarried after a spouse has willfully abandoned you and God has given you a desire to be married would be bondage and God does not want that.

So, from a remarriage perspective, you are not marriage material if you don't have biblical grounds for a divorce. God esteems the institution of marriage with the utmost reverence—and He also hates divorce—so He has provided very specific guidelines about divorce and remarriage. When you don't meet God's guidelines, then you are not marriage material.

I Got A Divorce Before I Was Saved and Knew the Word of God!

God's mercy is abundant to those who divorced in ignorance of His will for marriage. God deals with you in light of your current relationship with Jesus Christ, and the blood of Jesus covers your sin and ignorance. God does hold accountable those who are saved and know God's Word and willfully divorce their spouse without Biblical grounds.

But I Got A Divorce after I Was Saved, and I Knew It Was Wrong!
(Must I Stay Single And Miserable The Rest Of My Life?!?)

If you divorced your spouse knowing you did not have biblical grounds for divorce—you just decided you did not want to be married anymore—then you need to know that God is a God of mercy and love. Any directive He gives comes from His heart of love and mercy. His commands are not harsh and abrasive. If God has commanded that you remain unmarried or, if possible, return to the spouse you divorced if that person is unmarried, God knows what is best, and you must trust His judgment. God never relegates someone to a life of misery. We chose misery by viewing God's command without taking into consideration His character. You willingly disobeyed God's Word, but God still loves you and forgives you, if you ask Him. He also restores your relationship with Him. "If we confess our sins, He is faithful and just to forgive us of our sins and to cleanse us from all unrighteousness" (1 John 1:9 NKJV). However, though you are forgiven, your actions still have consequences. One consequence is that you are not permitted to remarry. God's love for you is still the same, and if you will begin to view your single life as He views it (a gift, according to 1 Corinthians 7:7) then you can begin to embark on a journey marked by God's intimate involvement. God will remove the misery and provide you with fulfillment and productivity as an unmarried adult. Romans 8:28 says, "We are assured and know that God being a partner in their labor] all things work together and are [fitting into a plan] for good to and for those who love God and are called according to [His] design and purpose." God will take the mistakes, disobedient acts and bad decisions in your life and work them for good when you agree to love Him and live your life according to His purposes and plans. If you find yourself in this situation, life has not ended; it has just begun if you yield to God and let Him have His way. Although God's way may seem hard, He loves you and He knows what is best for you, if you trust Him.

If you choose to commit adultery by remarrying, as many people do, God is merciful and forgiving, but there is always a consequence to disobedience. Remember that if you remarry and you did not fix the problems that caused the first divorce, the same type of marriage will probably occur again. That is probably why the divorce statistics are even higher for remarriages.

My Divorce Left Me Traumatized

Divorcees typically suffer tremendous emotional trauma and require significant healing. Those who fail to experience total and complete healing are not marriage material. If you are still wounded by your divorce, it would be unwise and even dangerous for you to take that unresolved pain and trauma into another relationship. God has provided the healing power of His Word and the comfort of the Holy Spirit to navigate you through this trauma, if you submit to the process. Many times people don't want to deal with the pain or the issues that led to the divorce and so they don't submit to the healing process. This is true of any significant relationship break-up. If you have not been healed, you are not ready to get married.

The most effective way to receive healing is through God's anointing, as described in Isaiah 61:1-3:

THE SPIRIT of the Lord God is upon me, because the Lord has anointed and qualified me to preach the Gospel of good tidings to the meek, the poor, and afflicted; He has sent me to bind up and heal the brokenhearted, to proclaim liberty to the [physical and spiritual] captives and the opening of the prison and of the eyes to those who are bound, To proclaim the acceptable year of the Lord [the year of His favor] and the day of vengeance of our God, to comfort all who mourn, To grant [consolation and joy] to those who mourn in Zion—to give them an ornament (a garland or diadem) of beauty instead of ashes, the oil of joy instead of mourning, the garment [expressive] of praise instead of a heavy, burdened, and failing spirit—that they may be called oaks of righteousness [lofty, strong, and magnificent, distinguished for

uprightness, justice, and right standing with God],
the planting of the Lord, that He may be glorified.

Divorcees often have to deal with depression, despair,
rejection and failure, suicidal tendencies, soul ties and
emotional trauma, unfulfilled sexual desires, loneliness and
financial difficulty. These issues must be dealt with before
you enter into a new relationship. A new marriage partner
will not heal you and solve these problems; they will only
complicate your life and add additional problems. If you
are still traumatized, and your life is marked by a rejection
mindset, then you can't appropriately interact with a new
spouse. If you are still emotionally attached to your spouse
even though you have a divorce contract that says you are
free, then you must be released from that soul tie. If your
finances are depleted as a result of getting a divorce, then
you should trust God and apply Kingdom financial principles to get your finances in order.

After almost seven years, my first marriage ended in
divorce due to blatant adultery. I remember agonizing in
prayer and seeking God's direction when it became apparent
that my first husband was unfaithful. I told God that if He
wanted me to stand in faith for Him to restore my marriage
He had to give me the grace I did not have in myself. I felt I
was in a no-win situation. One day God spoke these words
to me from 2 Corinthians 12:9: "My grace is sufficient for
you." (NKJV) Realizing that, and seeing no willingness in
my first husband to change his immoral behavior, I filed
for a divorce. It was the most painful and devastating time
in my life. Initially I thought, like so many divorcees, the
answer to my pain is a new relationship. But God did not
permit me to act on such unwise thinking. Over the next
ten years after that traumatic experience, God healed me of
the emotional trauma, purged me of the rejection, shame,
forgiveness and bitterness and prepared me to be marriage

material again. This healing and preparation took time and diligent responsive obedience. I had to give the Holy Spirit permission to deal with all the issues that caused me to marry unwisely the first time, as well as the trauma and devastation the divorce brought. When I remarried, I not only had biblical grounds to do so, I also had been healed of the trauma the first marriage and divorce had caused. God had made me into marriage material.

Race and Culture

Being of a different race, or coming from a different culture than the person you want to marry does not disqualify you as marriage material, but it may be challenging to the marriage if you don't respect understand and accept the cultural differences. The Kingdom principles of marriage should override cultural differences. Julius is a Nigerian, and I am an African-American. Things I had been told about Nigerian men before marrying my husband caused me to be concerned. I had heard Nigerian men were domineering, controlling and could never be satisfied with one wife. My husband very quickly changed my thinking on this matter by demonstrating that his life was not influenced by the culture he was born and raised in but by the culture of the Kingdom of God he now lives in. He lives his life in accordance with God's Word and not Nigerian culture. He is not domineering or controlling, but he loves me as Christ loves the church and is giving and kind. He serves me as a leader instead of dominating me as a leader. He is constantly seeking to make sure I become all that God wants me to be for his Kingdom. Julius's leadership is the reason why you are reading this book today. In our home he does not demand that I fix him food, he helps me prepare the food or cleans up after I prepare the food. When I am involved in housecleaning, many times he will stop what he is doing, to see if he can offer me assistance.

Julius still holds onto some of his culture's ways, including the food and, on special occasions, the attire. I have adapted to the attire and enjoy from time to time dressing in the native Nigerian dress. I am still learning to enjoy the food, but he eats it whenever he wants to, without forcing me to cook or eat it. I don't try to make him an American, and he doesn't try to make me a Nigerian. We respect our cultural differences.

Marrying someone of a different race because you believe that race is more qualified to be marriage material is unwise. Some African-Americans seem to think a white person will be a better marriage partner. Race is not the criteria to judge readiness for marriage. Marrying a certain race will not give you a successful marriage; only marrying a person that is marriage material will do this.

Chapter 18

Assess Yourself

To help you determine if you are marriage material I am providing an assessment tool. I placed this assessment toward the end of the book rather than the beginning so that you would have a greater understanding and appreciation of each criterion. This assessment has been designed to give you an opportunity to examine yourself against criteria that qualify you as marriage material. Transparency and honesty are essential in order for this self-evaluation to be meaningful. If you will be honest as you respond yes or no to each criteria this assessment will help you understand what areas you need to work on in order to prepare for marriage.

ARE YOU MARRIAGE MATERIAL ASSESSMENT

CRITERIA	YES	NO
Are you saved?		
Are you miserable about being single?		

CRITERIA	YES	NO
Are you anxious about a marriage partner?		
Do you have a healthy self-esteem based on what God's Word says about you?		
Is every man or woman you meet viewed as possible marriage partner?		
Have you discovered your specific purpose and destiny (God's reason for putting you on the earth?)		
Are you in debt, or do you have bad credit?		
Are you open and able to communicate your feelings?		
Do you live in obedience to authority figures God has placed in your life?		
Do you have a church and the support of a pastor?		
Are you a giver?		
Do you have a regular and effective prayer life?		
Do you have a regular time you spend in God's Word?		
Are you able to quickly forgive those who mistreat you?		
Is your sexual drive under control?		

CRITERIA	YES	NO
Are you masturbating on a regular basis?		
Are you looking at pornography?		
If you are a widow are you looking for an exact replica of your deceased spouse?		
Are you able to think pure thoughts about men or women or are you plagued with uncontrollable sexual thoughts?		
Are you obese?		
Are you shabby in appearance?		
Do you have significant health challenges?		
Do you have trouble making commitments?		
Do you have a job?		
Do you have a car or appropriate transportation?		
Do you have a growing savings account?		
Do you tithe 10% of your income to the Lord's work?		
Do your children want you to be married?		
Are your children secure and stable?		

CRITERIA	YES	NO
Have you been healed of emotional trauma associated with a divorce or other significant relationship breakup?		
Do you have Biblical grounds for remarriage?		
Do you know God's purpose for marriage?		
Are you lonely?		
Do you have hobbies or interests that you enjoy?		
Do you have strong friendships?		
Do you recognize God's voice?		
Are you jealous of others when they get married?		

Remember, God is not looking for you to be perfect when He sends your mate, but he does expect you to be ready. Also remember, God in his sovereignty could decide that He is ready to send you a marriage partner, even though you have difficulty in some of these areas. That is God's choice. But if God does not make that choice, then keep preparing yourself. God's preparation process depends on the number of problem areas you have, how well you respond to God's preparation process and the role your marriage will play in God's overall Kingdom agenda. As I stated earlier, God took almost fourteen years to prepare me for Julius. I now know it took so long because I had lots of problems that needed to be addressed and also because of the responsibility God has entrusted my husband and me within the Kingdom.

Chapter 19

I Am Not Marriage Material,
What Should I Do?

B y now, you probably have a pretty good idea whether you are marriage material. If you can be honest and admit that you are not marriage material, then what should you do? If you desire to be married and you are not marriage material, give your desire to God and ask Him to confirm His will for your life and prepare you for His will. God will answer that prayer. If God wants you married, He knows how to prepare you for marriage. God will mold you into the person you need to be for the marriage partner He has for you.

Don't seek to be married, seek to be successful at being single, and in the process God will prepare you for marriage. If you are not financially stable, work on improving your finances; if you are spiritually deficient in your study of God's Word and spending time in prayer, develop your relationship with the Lord. If your sexual drive is out of control, develop the fruit of the Spirit self-control. Begin to monitor your sexual behavior and eliminate those activities that stimulate your sexual drive, such as provocative movies and television or seductive music. If you are a sex addict seek out deliverance. Working on your problem areas will enhance your single life and prepare you for marriage. Successful single adults make the best marriage partners.

If you have discovered that you have a desire for marriage but you are not marriage material, I do not recommend dating. Dating may hinder the preparation process. You may develop pre-mature emotional attachments that you are not prepared to handle. Dating should be reserved for those who know they are marriage material and are in the process of preparing for marriage. My personal definition of dating is "an activity done in a safe, protected environment by two people of the opposite sex who believe God has spoken to them about making a marriage commitment to one another." In my opinion, people who date should actually meet many of the same criteria as those desiring to be married.

Also remember that readiness, not perfection, is the necessary element to qualify you as marriage material. Readiness means you are prepared to handle the responsibility of marriage, and this book has outlined what it takes to make you ready. Don't be overwhelmed or discouraged if you have discovered that there are several areas of your life that disqualify you right now. Remember, God loves you and is more committed to your success and making you into marriage material than you are. The Holy Spirit will impart to you wisdom and grace to prepare you for God's best.

Chapter 20

I Am Marriage Material, What Should I Do?

If, after reading this far in the book, you believe that you are ready to be married, then God recognizes your readiness and will direct your path. In addition to a God-molded desire and a genuine readiness, you must take into consideration God's overall plan for your life and God's timing. Proverbs 19:21 states, "Many plans are in a man's mind, but it is the Lord's purpose for him that will stand." Remember back in chapter eight I dealt with destiny and established that God has pre-determined our lives. This includes our marital status. God knows better than you, your readiness for marriage. He has been intimately involved in the preparation process, and He will bring you to His marriage partner for you in His time. Your responsibility is to trust God and enjoy the awesome gift of singleness He has entrusted you with.

Your life should be marked by fulfillment, contentment, success, significance, satisfaction and sexual purity. You should be developing your full potential within your single life. You should be satisfied to the point that you are at peace with your life, even though your every desire is not fully realized. You should be developing and growing in what God has called you to do. You should be consistently striving to live sexually pure in thought, word and deed. You should be having influence and impact within your sphere of influence that could be your local church, community, mission field, business or corporate America.

    Knowing you're ready for marriage but seeing no available prospects should not produce worry and anxiety, but rather a confident trust in your faithful God. You could be waiting for any number of reasons. Your future spouse may not be ready. God may still be molding their character, teaching them how to manage money, or cultivating leadership and submission skills. You don't want your future marriage partner until God has completed the preparation process. God completed the preparation process in Adam and completely formed Eve before He brought them together, and He will do the same for you.

    You may still be waiting, even though you're ready for marriage, because you have not yet completed your kingdom assignment while single. Callings, kingdom assignments and usage of God-given gifts are not reserved for marriage. Mary, the Mother of Jesus, had an assignment from God that she could accomplish only while single. God had predetermined for her to be Jesus' mother. In order for that to occur, she had to be a virgin and get pregnant by the Holy Spirit. This had to happen before she married Joseph.

    God wants you to know and begin to operate in your kingdom assignment while single. If God chooses to keep you single for a long time, you should enter marriage with a track record of Kingdom productivity. Maybe, while single, God will call you to start a business. And then you will bring into your marriage a successful business venture that gives you an opportunity to assist in financing the gospel. God did this with Boaz before he married Ruth. Boaz was a successful businessman before he married Ruth. He had cash and character. Maybe God will send you to the mission field and you will provide compassion and provision for many hurting children and this will prepare you for parenting your own family. Maybe God will develop your prayer life by calling you to spend significant time in intercession for your family, and then, because you pray, many of your unsaved family members will accept Jesus Christ as their personal Lord and Savior. You then bring proven intercession skills into your marriage and provide a powerful prayer covering that the forces of hell will not be able to attack and destroy. God may call you to start a ministry while you are single, and the skill and anointing you develop will be necessary to ensure that you are prepared for the destiny God has ordained for your marriage. Your single life should be marked by productivity and impact. The productivity and accomplishments of your single life will serve as building blocks for a solid marriage foundation. You should not bring lust, debt, misery and frustration with the single life to the wedding altar and your new marriage.

If you have become intimate with God while single, you should love the Lord and have a desire to please Him. You should be more concerned about God's kingdom than you are about getting married. That means you want to make sure you have accomplished everything that God pre-arranged for you to accomplish while single. Every good work associated with your single life should be accomplished. Remember what Ephesians 2:10 says, "For we are God's [own] handiwork (His workmanship), recreated in Christ Jesus, [born anew] that we may do those good works which God predestined (planned beforehand) for us [taking paths which He prepared ahead of time], that we should walk in them [living the good life which He prearranged and made ready for us to live]." Your single life, as well as your married life, carries with it good works. God wants to make sure you enter marriage with a testimony of having had a fulfilled life and having a sense that you accomplished every good work God wanted you to accomplish while single.

You should want to achieve your Kingdom assignment *before* you seek to fulfill your own marriage desires. Matthew 6:33 says, "But more than anything else, put God's work first and do what he wants. Then the other things will be yours as well" (CEV). God is not intentionally withholding a husband or wife from you. God is concerned about His Kingdom and will meet every need you have—including a spouse—when you put His kingdom first.

So, if you know you are marriage material and yet you still find yourself waiting, God has a good reason. Ask Him and He may choose to reveal it to you. Also, be confidently assured that God will not withhold your marriage partner when you are ready. Continue to accomplish the good works associated with your single life and at your appointed time God will orchestrate a divine connection with you and your marriage partner!

Chapter 21

Seal It With Prayer

Are You Marriage Material? Based on your response, I would like to provide you with some prayers. If you have a strong desire for marriage and yet realize you are not marriage material, you may be hurting. God knows that, He cares and He wants to help you through this difficult time. He has led you to this point of awareness and pain to keep you from making mistakes that would be even more painful than the pain you are experiencing right now. As you trust Him and obey He will prepare you for marriage and give you a life of fulfillment while waiting. I encourage you to pray the following prayer:

Prayer For Those Who Are Not Yet Marriage Material

Father,

After reviewing the material in this book, I believe the Holy Spirit has been able to point out areas in my life that reveal that I am not yet marriage material. I have already shared with you, Father, my desire to one day be married.

I repent if I have allowed that desire to become an idol and rule my thoughts and actions.

More than being married now I want to be in the center of your will, and so first I put my desire for a marriage partner on the altar. I recognize by doing this I can now begin to grow and experience all that you have planned for me. Make me into the man or woman of God that you planned for me to be from the foundations of the world. Let me begin to experience and partake of that awesome destiny that you predetermined for me to have. Call me into your awesome presence so that I can begin to cultivate intimacy with you. More than anything, I want to experience the fullness of joy and the pleasures of your right hand that the Bible promises including peace, productivity, prosperity fulfillment and wisdom that can only be found in your presence.

Help me to become a successful single who has a life marked by undivided and undistracted devotion to you, sexual purity, financial success and your calling to advance your Kingdom. Father, if it is in your perfect plan for me to be married one day, reveal it to me and begin to prepare me for marriage. Make me into marriage material and provide me with a Godly spouse whom I can come together with and cause your name to be glorified as we demonstrate together the relationship that Christ is to have to the church.

Father, I give you permission to deal with those areas in my life that currently disqualifies me as marriage material. If your dealings with me appear to be painful and hard, then help me to realize that your actions are always motivated by a heart of love and that you only want me to have your best. I trust you, Holy Spirit—during those seasons when I am being pruned, purged and chastised—that your grace will be ever present and all sufficient.

In the meantime, Father, I just want you to know I intend to grow in my ability to experience complete satisfaction and fulfillment by being in relationship with you. In you I live, in you I move, and in you I have my being.

If I am a single parent, Lord, while you are preparing me for a marriage partner, prepare my children for a new parent. I make a commitment to them, in your presence, to never enter into a marriage relationship that will negatively impact my relationship with them or negatively impact their lives and destinies, and I trust you to ensure all their needs are met.

In Jesus Name.
Amen.

Prayer for Those Who Desire To Remarry But Don't Have A Biblical Grounds For Remarriage

If you have discovered while reading this book that remarriage is not an option for you according to God's Word, and yet the desire for marriage is still there, remember that God knows, He cares, and in this moment of what may be intense pain and confusion, He wants to direct your path, if you let him. Here is a prayer for you to pray.

Father,

I come to you and I find myself in this very difficult situation because of disobedience to your Word. I know your forgiving mercy covers my sin, and so I ask you for forgiveness, and by faith I believe that I receive your magnificent mercy. Your loving kindness is better than life itself.

Father, I also recognize that we reap what we sow, and even though I am forgiven, there are consequences to my sin, and I pray now that you will begin to empower me with your all-sufficient grace to accept those consequences.

The thought of not being able to marry again is more than I can bear right now, so help me to take comfort in the promise of your Word. You instruct me to trust you in my times of weakness, because in my weakness your strength is made perfect. I desperately need your strength to accept this fact right now. Help me to understand that your commands are designed to bring your joy into my life. Your loving kindness and mercy are eternal.

Help me to live with confident expectation and joyful anticipation about the future you have planned for me. Help me live according to Romans 8:28, which says, all things will work together for good in my life as I choose to love you with all my heart. And help me to demonstrate that love by my obedience to the direction you are giving me as I choose to live my life submitted to your purposes and plans.

As painful as my life is right now, help me to trust your character enough to know that this too will pass, and one day, as I seek to live a successful single life marked by undistracted devotion to you, I will experience fullness of joy and the pleasures of your right hand which include peace, productivity, prosperity fulfillment and wisdom. And even more important, you will take my tears and tragedies and turn them into a miraculous testimony that glorifies you.

In Jesus Name.
Amen

Prayer For Those God Has Called To Remain Unmarried

Father,

As I pray over the matter of marriage, I sense that you are directing me to remain unmarried for Kingdom purposes. I am honored and humbled at this awesome call and direction you have placed on my life. I endeavor to live my life in undivided, undistracted devotion to you, and experience as the apostle Paul did, the revelation and impact that comes from the unmarried lifestyle in your Kingdom.

I thank you that you have given me sufficient grace to live alone and to live holy. You are my marriage partner, Father, and you are more than enough to bring me fulfillment and fruitfulness.

In Jesus Name.
Amen

Prayer For Those Who Are Marriage Material But Have Not Met God's Choice

If you read this book and you received the confirmation you needed to continue to stand in faith for your man or woman of God, here is a prayer for you.

Father,

I thank you so much for sending this book as a confirmation that indeed you have ordained for me to be married and that I do qualify as marriage material. While I am waiting, help me to not grow weary in well doing so that in my appointed season I shall experience the very best marriage you can possibly give me. Holy Spirit, constantly remind me that I need patience, so that after I have done God's will I might receive the promise. And give me the grace to demonstrate my patience by keeping my joy strong. Help me to continuously praise and rejoice, knowing that you are faithful. Holy Spirit, keep me sensitive to your promptings so that when you are ready to begin to orchestrate my divine connection I am ready and prompt to obey your guidance, just like Isaac and Rebecca, Salmon and Rahab and Boaz and Ruth.

While I am waiting, let me take full advantage of the opportunity I have for undistracted fellowship with you. Remind me that, even when I experience the best that marriage can offer me, it will never be as awesome as the intimate relationship I am developing with you.

While waiting for my mate, Father, I thank you for allowing me to experience successful single living.

If I am a single parent, while my children are waiting for their new parent, may they be filled with faith, marked by patience and joy, and may they experience no lack because you are being faithful to ensure their every need is met.

In Jesus Name
Amen

About The Author

D ebbie Adebayo is Founder and President of Singles Pleasing the Lord, a ministry that God is using to prepare single adults to impact His Kingdom. The ministry meets the needs of unmarried adults, spiritually, mentally, physically, economically and socially. The Ministry of Singles Pleasing The Lord hosts seminars, conferences, workshops and social events. The ministry also makes available a free online newsletter called the Single Link and, for partners of the ministry, a quarterly publication titled the Single Perspective.

Debbie was unmarried for twenty-four years of her adult life. She experienced the challenges of the single life being single and never married until she was 28. Then she was separated and divorced after seven years of marriage. Debbie raised her teenage stepson as a single parent after her marriage ended. She has a track record with the single life and has discovered the principles of successful single living.

She hosts a radio broadcast and talk show for single adults and a television show called "Living Single God's Way and Loving It" that currently airs on radio stations and cable channels in the Chicagoland area. Her communication of Biblical truth is genuine, transparent, vibrant and practical. God has opened doors for her to minister across the country and in Africa.

For over 17 years she served faithfully in her local church in a variety of positions, including Director of the Sunday School, Director of the Building Fund, Intercessory Prayer Leader and Neighborhood Minister. She has attended the Kings Seminary in Van Nuys, California, and the Marilyn Hickey Correspondence Bible School. Debbie also is a registered nurse and has a Masters Degree in Business Administration. In July of 2005 she married Julius Adebayo, pastor of Cornerstone Outreach Center and, in addition to directing the Ministry of Singles Pleasing The Lord, she serves along side her husband in this ministry.

To contact the author or for additional information about the Ministry of Singles Pleasing The Lord visit www.singles-pleasingthelord.com, write P.O. Box 924 West Chicago, IL 60186, call 630 513-0038 or email debra.adebayo@singles-pleasingthelord.com.

Additional Teaching Materials
By Debbie Adebayo

(These teachings are available on audiocassette and CD)

Lord I Am So Tired of Being Lonely
Relationship Building and Dating
Single Parent Workshop: Help For Those
Raising Children Alone
Getting Your Life Back On Track
Somebody Stop Me From Having Sex
If I Can't Have Sex…What Can I Have?
Singles and Money
Single, Sex, Money and God's Purpose For Your Life
How To Believe God For A Marriage Partner
Praying Single Women Producing Powerful Single Men
The Love Life of The Single Adult
Why In The World Am I Single Anyway?
Principles of Successful Single Living
Lead Me Not Into Temptation
The Power of The Praying Single Adult
Singles and Sex
The Wedding Package – Includes Debbie Adebayo's
Wedding DVD

You can order these teaching materials by visiting: www.
singlespleasingthelord.com, calling 630 513-0038 or
writing P.O. Box 924 West Chicago, IL

"Being single is not a problem to be solved
but a gift to be enjoyed."

Printed in the United States
144885LV00002B/76/A